The Amazonian Pharmacy
of Don Ignacio Duri

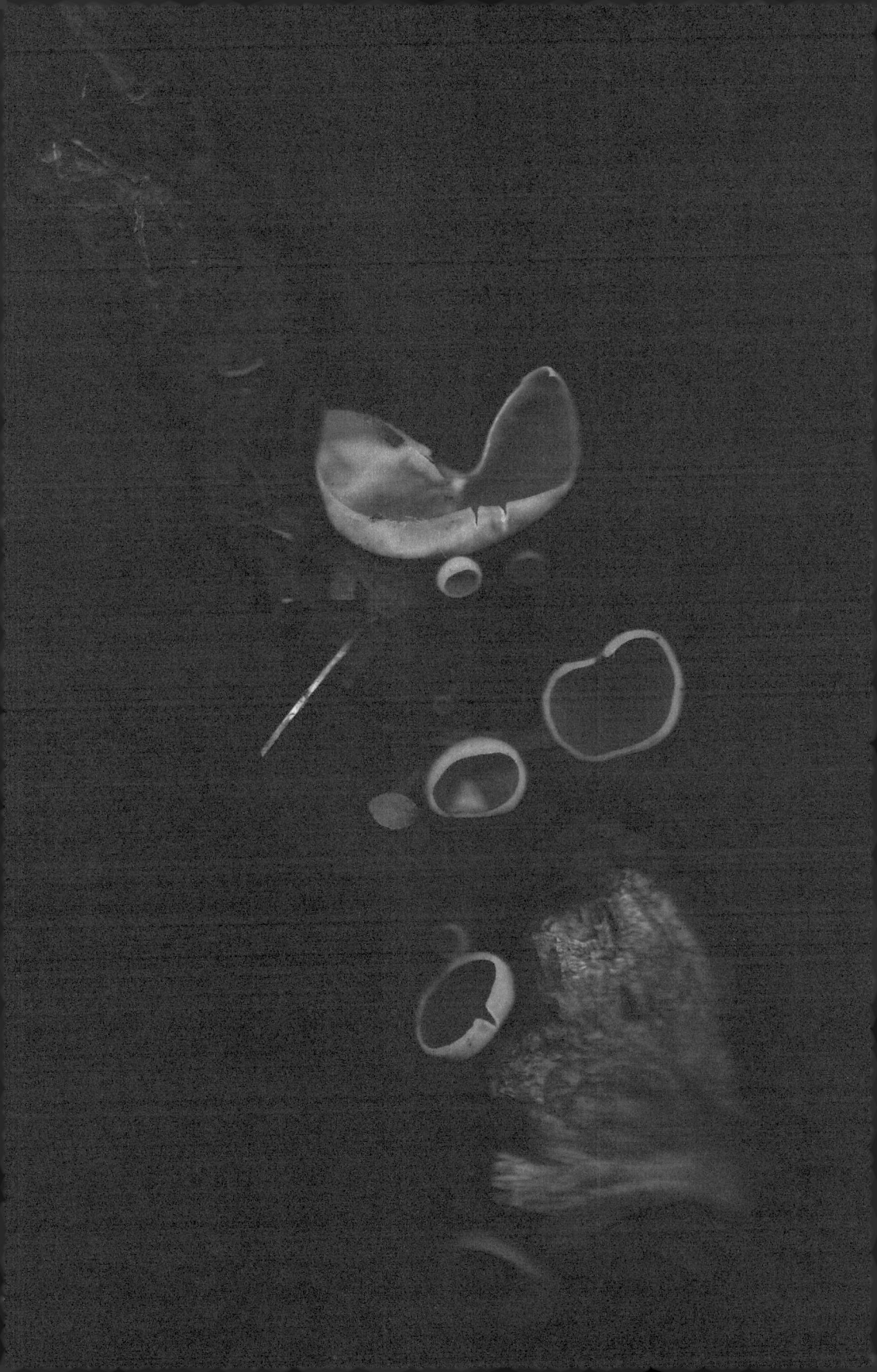

The Amazonian Pharmacy of Don Ignacio Duri

Robin Van Loon & Camila Villalobos

Translated By Elise Van Der Heijden

Half title page: *Cookeina* mushrooms, Blair Butterfield
Title page: Caña caña (*Costus* sp.), Maise McNeice

© 2024 by Robin Van Loon & Camila Villalobos
Botanical illustrations © 2023 by Maisie McNeice
Plant portrait photographs © 2023 by Blair Butterfield
Drawing of Don Ignacio's house © 2023 by Francisco Aros
Photograph of Don Ignacio harvesting chacruna © 2023 by Nicholas Hardy
Portrait photograph of Don Ignacio © 2023 by Carolina Gutierrez
Photograph of Don Ignacio seated before ceremony © 2023 Oscar Miró-Quesada
All other photographs © 2023 by Robin Van Loon

ISBN paperback: 979-8-9905010-0-3

Cover photograph: Don Ignacio harvesting chacruna, by Nicholas Hardy
Cover art: Plant portrait of rubber tree, by Blair Butterfield
Cover design: Panagiotis Lampridis
Interior Design/Typesetting: Rebecca LeGates

Orders, inquiries, and correspondence should be addressed to:

Camino Verde
95 Marthas Point Rd.
Concord, MA 01742
info@caminoverde.org

Printed in the United States of America

10 9 8 7 6 5 4 3 2 1

Table of Contents

Cashapona (Socratea exorrhiza) →

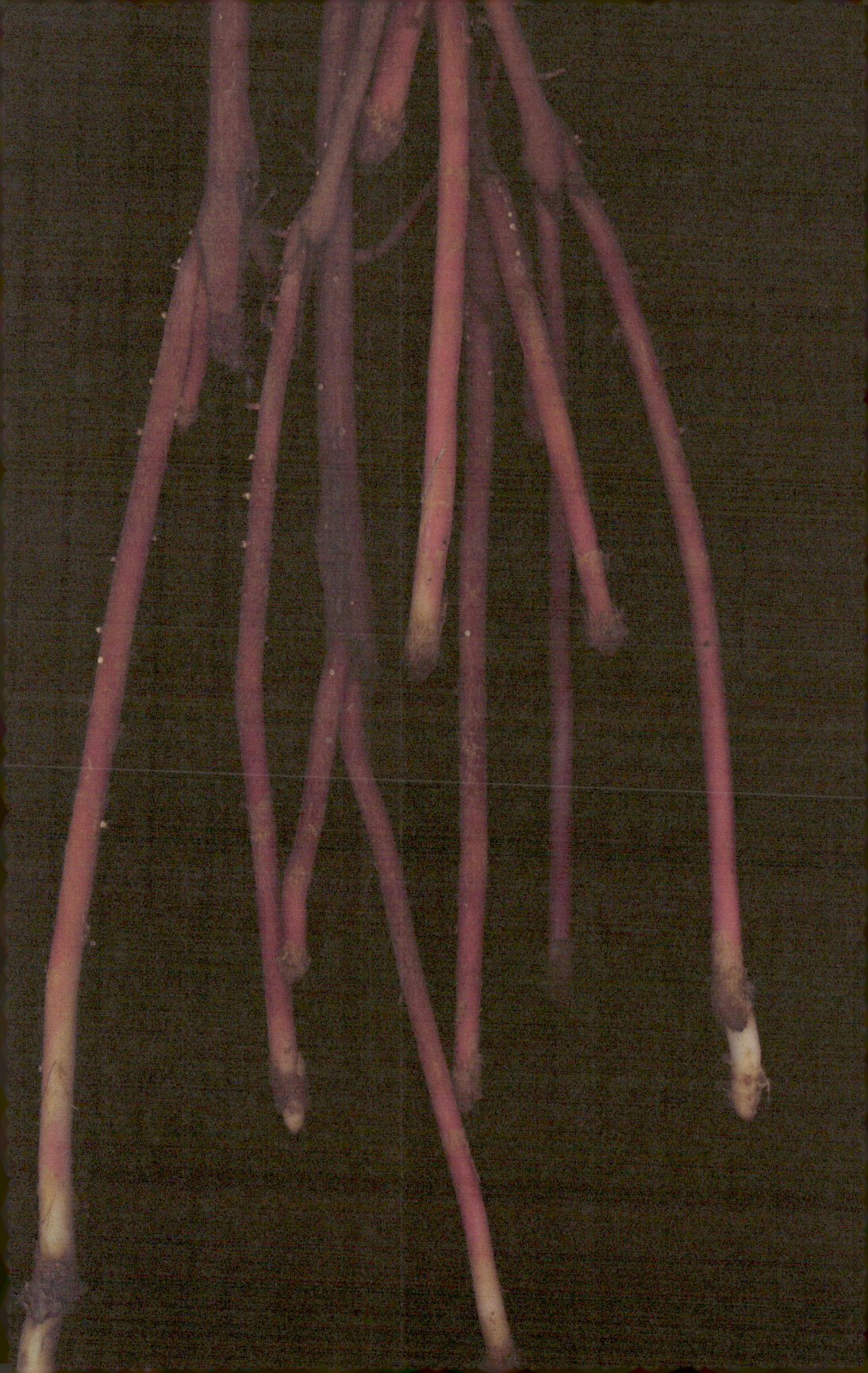

When you look at the forest, all the plants,
you're looking at the shelves of a pharmacy,
remedies of different sizes and colors, up there, down
here, each one with its label. You pick up a plant and
you read what that plant is for. And each remedy,
each pharmacy bottle, has its price tag. Its price is
how strict you have to diet. How long you're going to
diet it, that's how much the remedy costs.

—Don Ignacio

← Huasaí roots (*Euterpe precatoria*)

Don Ignacio harvesting sanganga leaves (*Pariana* sp.) in 2011 →

Prologue

Don Ignacio Duri Palomeque was born in 1930 in the Bolivian Amazon. He was one of the founders of the native community of Infierno, located in the department of Madre de Dios, Peru, where he lived and practiced as a healer and shaman for over 40 years.

The oral recordings that form the content of this book were made between 2007 and 2017 at Don Ignacio Duri's house, at his request and with his blessing.

Whoever passed by the home of Don Ignacio could attest to his simplicity and humility. He was a unique human being. Magical, modest, enigmatic, and with a grand, intelligent sense of humor. It's difficult to describe him in only a few words. His silence, and the evocation of tranquility—these were some of the traits that characterized his presence. So, the moments when he was inspired to share a small part of his long and singular life in this world—and in other worlds through which he also moved—were gifts to be honored. This book is a compilation of many such moments over many years, recorded in audio at Don Ignacio's house, where we, the authors, too had arrived—like many others from many parts of the world—in search of help and healing, via the knowledge and connection that this man of the jungle held with ayahuasca and the plants of the Amazon rainforest.

The material compiled over the space of almost a decade was transcribed and edited as little as possible, in order to bring the reader closer to the plants invoked and to this character narrating a part of his life story. We originally contemplated preserving the transcriptions in pure form, but as we wrote out the text, we

← Ayahuasca (*Banisteriopsis caapi*)

kept noticing the distracting repetition of filler words and idiomatic expressions. In order to make his stories scan for a wider Spanish-reading (and now, English-reading) audience, we had to introduce some few and minor modifications to the literally transcribed text, slightly adjusting its syntax and composition. The intervention of the text wasn't an easy decision; as a matter of fact, it was our last recourse. This, with the aim of obtaining a more fluid reading experience while avoiding the loss of the identity and voice of Don Ignacio in his own story—a delicate and sensitive task, which has left us with more than one remaining concern even now.

The goal of publishing this book was not to bring to light material of a scientific nature or to create a reference covering the complex topic of shamanism. Nor is it a book of fantastical stories. What we have here is a text which, due to its origin and format, doesn't allow itself to be cleanly inserted into a single traditional literary genre, nor can it be explained solely through the lens of western empirical rationality. The publication of Don Ignacio's stories was a way in which he hoped for his knowledge and wisdom to be preserved in time and memory. It was his intention that, through his voice, a small, perhaps tiny piece of the plant heritage silently held in the forests of the Peruvian Amazon would not be lost in oblivion.

In parallel, this book is an invitation for people with hearts, minds and souls willing to receive and value its contents. An invitation to enter the everydayness of a simple story filled with magic; to cross through the doorways of dreamlike and ceremonial universes which are portrayed in it; to get closer to a sacred understanding of plants as active agents within the context they inhabit—conscious beings with personalities that distinguish them (good and bad, like everything of which the universe is composed). This is the story of a farmer of the Amazon. A small reflection of the everyday life of a culture that still preserves ancestral practices in relation to the natural environment which that culture inhabits, as well as evidence of historical processes that marked these abundant lands exploited for their resources.

On June 18, 2020, Don Ignacio died at the age of 89. It is difficult to conceive of this home in the jungle without him. With his passing we have lost a marvelous human being, as well as a foundational representative of the local shamanic tradition. This book is, to a certain extent and in a symbolic manner, a small transmission of his knowledge.

—Camila Villalobos Contreras

A Note on the Transcription

To diverge as little as possible from Don Ignacio's original words, their music and their meaning: this was our goal during the transcription and editing of this book's manuscript.

Inevitably, both the "translation" from oral to written form and the translation from Spanish to English resulted in the introduction of some few words added and others subtracted, always performed with care and in the interest of lending the oral transmission a more fluid reading experience. The authors' poetic license resulted in the ordering of the book's chapters, interspersed with brief stand-alone plant profiles presented in alphabetical order.

The text includes other clarifying elements to facilitate the reading, such as the incorporation of text boxes containing brief explanatory notes on certain terms fundamental to the shamanic practices conducted by Don Ignacio. The inclusion of footnotes also enabled us to elucidate the content further, mainly by offering scientific names of the plants and animals mentioned by common name by Don Ignacio, as well as geographical places and other references specific to the Peruvian Amazon.

The process of adding this information evolved from discussions among botany staff from the non-profit organization Camino Verde and between the authors of the book. Based on our time spent in learning with Don Ignacio, we have tried to find words similar to the ones he would have used to shed some light on certain local shamanic practices. We have not attempted to transmit the full depth of these terms' meanings in this book, but rather have designed these additions as a complement to the text.

The illustrations illuminating this edition are by Blair Butterfield and Maisie McNeice, both past botanical artists in residence at Camino Verde. The English translation was crafted by Elise van der Heijden in close collaboration with the authors.

← Azúcar Huayo resin lumps (*Hymenaea courbaril*)

How can we start this off? With the story of me drinking ayahuasca? From the time I started drinking, right? Alright, let me think a bit about how my tragedy with all that began.

—Don Ignacio

From Pando,[1] Bolivia, from Porvenir, that's the country where I was born; that's where I was a kid. I came to Peru from Bolivia in 1946, at sixteen years old. I was supposed to join the army in Bolivia at seventeen, but I came over here. You see, my mom started seeing a Peruvian man, and the Peruvian brought us over to Peru. That's the reason I'm here; if not, I would still be in Bolivia. He took us over on the condition that we enter school, but in the end, I didn't go to school here. I started working on the farm.[2] In Bolivia, I was only in school for five months. They say education used to be good before, here in Peru, but now education has hit rock bottom and it's all a business.

---

1. Department of Pando, Bolivian Amazon.
2. Don Ignacio uses the word *chacra*, from the Quechua for farm (field), usually small, family-owned, including trees, biodiverse. Known as *chaco* in Bolivia.

← Chacruna (*Psychotria viridis*)

When we arrived here, the Peruvian came to start a school where the Manguaré[3] is now located. Over there, on that corner was the school that he started so that my sisters could get an education.

I had been in my mother's belly for three months when my legitimate father died. I was born in the custody of Vargas; Felipe Vargas was the name of the guy my mother was with when I was born. Vargas raised me for two years and then he also died. Vargas left two children behind, and then the Peruvian met my mom; they got together, and he took us to his house. He had been working in rubber tapping but later he got into agriculture. We had people working for us; we used to grow sugar cane and coffee. We had eight hectares of sugar cane and good coffee plantations; that's where we lived, harvesting coffee, still peeling it in a wooden mortar,[4] grinding it by hand. They would carry off eight sacks of peeled coffee beans at a time; they would hand select the coffee that would be taken. All of it planted, it's not a little piece of land. I guess that must be why I like coffee.

We also had animals, cattle. When we came from Bolivia, I think he left his brother like six head. The animals we brought later died; there were eleven heifers, and they would eat weeds![5] There wasn't any grass, you know. The cows would knock down cetico trees;[6] that's what they would eat. When there were no more ceticos left, they had nothing else to eat. The animals died one by one and then there were none left. The thought didn't cross the old man's mind, to give them some pastureland, right?

---

3. Recreation center in the city of Puerto Maldonado, named after the traditional log drum (*manguaré*) played in the communal long houses or *malocas* of various Amazonian peoples.
4. *Pilón*, a type of wooden mortar used to pound, crush, and grind grains and other foods.
5. The word employed, *purma*, refers to the weeds from a secondary forest which typically grow from abandoned farm parcels. Certain pioneer tree species such as the cetico mentioned are characteristic of the purma successional ecosystem, on its way slowly toward the distinct species mix and forest structure typical of a primary (undisturbed) forest.
6. A fast-growing pioneer tree species. *Cecropia* sp. (family Cecropiaceae).

There was a ranch right next door; there was a man called Tobías Ramírez that had a pasture right there.

Puerto Maldonado was tiny back then; it was just a few blocks around the main square. How Puerto Maldonado has grown since then! Bah… That whole area where the Mercado Modelo[7] is now, all that was a bamboo patch![8] Up past the prison, that was all a swamp. That's where the shirui[9] would gather, in those pools. They're no longer there now, those pools.

Been here since '46. Geeze, Maldonado has gotten so big. And it's continuing to grow, eh?

---

7. The main market of Puerto Maldonado.
8. A *pacal* is a bamboo thicket, an area of impenetrable and very thorny vegetation, mainly consisting of spiny Amazonian bamboo known as paca, of the genus *Guadua* (Poaceae).
9. Fish species found in seasonal pools and wetlands. *Callichthys callichthys* (family Callichthydae).

ONE

The First Ceremony

When I was discharged from the army in 1951, I was twenty years old.[10] That's when I went to the Bolivian border, to the Manuripi River to tap shiringa,[11] rubber. There, I met a man who was from Iquitos. His name was Enrique Pacaya.

One afternoon, I stopped by the house of another rubber tapper and there was the old man, cooking ayahuasca.[12] I was one hour away from the Manuripi River and I had to cross it[13] swimming.

"Where are you goin', Duri?" he asks me.

"I'm going to get food, I don't have any," I say to him.

"There aren't any canoes on the river," he says, "you'll get there at dusk. You might even jump into the river and some critter could grab you. It's better if you stay. I'm cooking ayahuasca. Let's drink some!" the old man says to me.

"Really?"

"Yeah, stay!" he says to me, "Something could happen to you. There aren't any canoes on the river."

---

10. Don Ignacio served in the Peruvian army. He avoided military service in Bolivia by moving to Peru, but once there he served at the local army base.
11. Process by which latex is extracted from the rubber tree, or shiringa, *Hevea brasiliensis* (Euphorbiaceae), via diagonal cuts made in the tree's bark. The extraction of rubber was historically of vital importance to the Amazonian economy.
12. Woody liana. *Banisteriopsis caapi* (Malpighiaceae).
13. He uses the word *chimbar*, a local phrase meaning to wade, swim, or boat to the other side of a river or lake.

← Cetico (*Cecropia* sp.)

"Alright then." I stayed.

He was cooking his ayahuasca just over there by the edge of the forest. Back then, they didn't cook it the way we cook it now; they cooked it for only two or three hours. But you have to drink a lot when it's cooked like that.

Eight o'clock arrived. There were eight people sitting in a circle. He gave each one of them a cup first and then he gave me one. The others were already "drunk"[14] after one cup. After twenty, twenty-five minutes they were already having visions, they were laughing, they were seeing girls, singing… Ayahuasca makes you want to sing and that's why you shouldn't forbid anyone to sing. Those who can, can sing, no problem.

I'm sitting there, listening to them. The old man is by my side and asks me, "And Duri," he says, "how are you doing?"

I reply, "Just fine, Don Enrique."

"Not feeling drunk?"

"No."

"Do you want some more?"

"Alright then," I tell him.

I accepted it from him. He gave me another cup and I drank it.

"The drunkenness won't take long to arrive when you've had two cups," he said to me.

Another twenty minutes went by.

"And Duri, how are you doing?"

"Fine, Don Enrique, I don't feel anything."

"Not feeling drunk?"

"Not at all."

"Do you want another cup?"

"Alright then."

Another cup, that makes three! I just went for it, damnit. He just sat there for a while longer and then he asks me again, "And

---

14. Don Ignacio is not alone in this phrasing, common among ayahuasqueros. The term *borrachera* or "drunkenness" is used to refer to the physical effects and the altered state of consciousness that is experienced from ingesting the decoction of ayahuasca.

Duri, nothing?"

"Nothing, Don Enrique," I said to him.

"Serve yourself! The pot is over there."

Alright then; I grabbed the cup. When I went to take the first sip, boom! Shoot, I don't even remember what I did with the cup. Man, the drunkenness came washing over me; I say to him: "Ooh…"

The old man was singing in his language, in Inca,[15] some *carnavales*[16] songs, and what pretty music! I've never seen anything like it to this day. He sang so pretty, like some kind of little bells. From there, in my vision I saw some girls inviting me to drink *chicha*;[17] I'm drinking with them, a frothy chicha in some cups, but where did those cups come from? I can't find cups like those—they were really pretty cups.

And there I was, with him. He told me to sing, and I was propped up against a wooden post, that's where I was, and I just opened my mouth and said, "Ah aah aaah…!"

That's all I did. A once-in-a-lifetime drunkenness took hold of me.

The old man sang *icaros** and told me to dance. That's when I saw myself dancing in the middle of the crowd. The old man sang a carnavales song, and I was number one at dancing out of everybody.

After that, in my vision we arrived at a *collpa*;[18] they took me to this large clay lick, a feeding place for animals. In the center there was a tree leaning to one side with a rope hanging down from it. Huge monkeys were using it to climb up, and then they came

---

15. Probably Quichua or Quechua, or possibly Asháninka.
16. *Carnavales* are a specific rhythm of song played at festivities of the same name, during the season of carnavales in Peru and other Catholic countries in South America.
17. *Chicha* is a term that normally refers to fermented beverages made from a variety of ingredients, typically served at community festivities throughout Peru. Incidentally, Don Ignacio often used chicha as a synonym for ayahuasca, which tends to ferment within days of being prepared and can often have a distinctly fermented taste.
18. Local term for clay lick, an ecologically important place where the soil is rich with mineral deposits where a range of animals come to feed.

* Ícaro

A term whose meaning varies by region, lineage, ethnicity, and according to the circumstances of use. The most common definitions of ícaro are a shamanic healing chant or a healing-oriented prayer. Depending on the context, the verb *icarear* means to bless or "cure" a remedy before serving it, an object before using it ceremonially, and/or to bless or pray on behalf of a person.

In the Peruvian Amazon, ícaros are primarily understood as songs or chants that belong to a curandera or curandero, melodic expressions of his or her personal spirit used to heal and guide patients or participants in ceremonies. The ícaros of shamans or shamanesses are representative of their healing abilities and channels through which their spiritual presence is transmitted. Ícaros are bestowed upon healers and apprentices directly from spirit through the concentration and spiritual effort associated with shamanic diets involving master plants ingested for learning and healing. In some instances, ícaros may be passed on from teacher to student rather than received directly from spiritual sources. In many Amazonian traditions, each plant is considered to have its song(s), and these are shared with the shaman as part of a learning process involving ceremonies, visions and dreams. The healer first comprehends the meaning and function of a given melody or song, then implements it as a tool of healing through the act of "ícaro-ing" (*icareando*).

Each ícaro has unique characteristics in terms of melody, intonation and use in ceremonial work, and each song offered by a given plant can produce different effects according to the spiritual functions it fulfills. Some ícaros are meant to call in the spirit of a plant or tree for protection and/ or healing, others to cure illness, or to initiate and protect a ceremony and the people who participate in it. There are even ícaros to give strength or serenity during a challenging healing process, among other purposes. Some ayahuasqueros mention that for each human illness—both physical and spiritual—there is a corresponding healing ícaro.

back down in the shape of people and started playing carnavales,[19] those people, all covered in mud. Oh, carnavales!

After that, she asked me, Ayahuasca said to me, "Why are you drinking? Are you going to learn?"

"Maybe," I told her.

"Keep going," she said to me.

Geeze, I sure saw pretty that time, damnit! That was the first time I took ayahuasca. I was in that state of drunkenness until four in the morning. That's why I say, if you boil ayahuasca for three hours, you have to drink lots, but you stay drunk until the morning. It's more potent, it's purer. Not anymore; by now we've practiced at it. It's cooked down to an essence now and it lasts four to five hours at most.

At four in the morning, I came to my senses. The old man was looking at me, and he says to me, "So Duri? How are you?"

"I've returned to my senses now, Don Enrique." I say to him.

My belly was like a bag of water; I couldn't wait for dawn. The sun came and I went into the forest; the forest was really close by. What a purgative that was, damnit. I come back and the old man was standing there by the stream and says to me, "Did it make you purge?"

"Yes," I say to him.

"Now you're going to bathe yourself and you're going to diet* for four days. Don't eat this, or this, all of it without salt, without sugar. Forget about women too," he says.

In the year 1952 I started to drink ayahuasca. Four years I stayed out there, tucked away in the rubber camp.[20] That's where I learned this. In 1951 I went there and in '55 I came out to vote for the late Prado, Manuel Prado, the first election I voted in.

For three years I took ayahuasca. I'd drink one night, then diet for fifteen, twenty days and only then would I drink again. I would drink again, diet for thirty days and so on; that's the diet,

---

19. One local tradition for carnavales involves a raucous game in which people throw mud, water, paint, etc., at members of the opposite sex as part of the celebrations.

20. He uses the word *gomal*, an agglomeration of rubber trees also known as a *shiringal*.

Dieta

"Diets" are a fundamental pillar of shamanic learning in the Amazon. "Dieting" a teacher plant involves various considerations of a physical and spiritual nature, including foregoing or abstaining from ordinary dietary, mental, and social habits. The objectives of diets include healing from an illness and learning from teacher plants. The term describes a process of preparing the body, mind, and spirit to better receive the plant or plants "dieted." In this sense, diets can be understood as a form of cleansing and purification, characterized by a specialized dietary regime – defined by the absence of salt, sugar, red meat, condiments, and acidic or pungent foods such as onions, garlic, and citrus fruits. The bland food consumed in limited quantities during a shamanic diet mainly consists of rice, plantains, cassava and some select types of meat and fish. The strictness and partic- ulars are linked to the purpose of the diet and fundamentally determined by the kind of plant that is being dieted.

The dieting process involves concentration, silence and solitude, as well as the frequent ceremonial ingestion of the plant(s) being dieted. Other essential components are social isolation, sexual abstinence and—as Don Ignacio affirmed in relation to male dieters—avoidance of menstruating women, as these encounters are understood to be potentially disorienting.

Amazonian shamanic adepts sometimes go on very long diets—of months or even years—in the depths and solitude of the forest. Dieting is an intense and personal process, which is why Don Ignacio described the diet as a kind of payment to the dieted plant, a form of compensating for the learning and healing granted by the plant(s) to the person dieting. Ignacio frequently indicated that properly carrying out a diet "should cost you," i.e., should not be experienced as easy. Proper dieting is thus a rigor- ous test of will that requires effort and intention on the part of the dieter.

Not respecting the diet, "cutting" or "breaking" it abruptly, can produce harmful consequences including physical and mental illness, effects oppo- site to those being sought. In this way, it is understood that a plant may work against (or "give *la contra*" to) the person dieting in the event that he/ she fails to show proper respect by honoring the strict terms of the diet.

you know. I worked rubber alone at my camp. I had hens; I had dogs. There were two hundred twenty rubber trees. I would go and slash my *estrada*[21] without having any breakfast; I would come back at ten in the morning, and then I would go back in at noon to pick up the "milk."[22] I would come back out at two in the afternoon; I'd smoke-cure[23] the rubber milk until four in the morning, and that's how I passed the time. I ate my *shivé*[24] unsweetened. I was never short on that. It was a pure food without any salt, without any fat, without any seasoning. That's what I ate.

When I came back from there, from Manuripi, well, I knew. I'd smoke my pipe and if I wanted to know about a girl, what her life was like, I would see it just like that in my dreams. Right now, I can't reach that level because here I'm surrounded by lots of people,[25] so I can't. But I know everything, what people's weak points are... I see it all in a heartbeat. If a girl's going to get married, if I want to cancel the wedding, I can do that right now. You learn all those sorts of things.

That's why I call out these ayahuasqueros that don't know anything. I asked Felipe Collantes[26] to do a love spell for me. I

---

21. Network of paths in the rainforest, usually made with the objective of harvesting or extracting forest resources, facilitating access to rubber or Brazil nut trees.
22. Colloquial way to refer to the resin or latex from a tree.
23. Process of drying the rubber from the shiringa tree using smoke to solidify it.
24. Typical jungle cereal, made from the kind of toasted cassava flour known as *fariña* in Peru (from the Portuguese *farinha*, meaning flour), mixed with water or the beverage made from the delicious, creamy ungurahui fruit (*Oenocarpus bataua*).
25. Shamanic learning and the diet require solitude. Don Ignacio means to imply that, by living in his community surrounded by people, his capacities as a healer have been reduced.
26. Felipe Collantes was one of Don Ignacio's few peers among traditional healers in Madre de Dios, though Collantes was the younger of the two by a significant margin. Of Shipibo descent, he managed an impressive range of ícaro melodies and was known locally as a powerful healer. On some few occasions, the two men worked together in healing ceremonies, but they could perhaps more properly be understood as rivals. Collantes passed away years before Don Ignacio.

also asked Panduro;[27] he's worked on me twice, but I still can't see any results. That's why I say it's no good being surrounded by people. That's why I can't see as far; but I understand it all, all of everything. I've tested all those ayahuasqueros that have taken ayahuasca with me by asking them to do a service for me, as they say, a binding spell[28] with a girl with the power of this plant, right? But these men, well they can't do it! They don't get what this science is.

I didn't go back again to Manuripi; I came to Puerto Maldonado. I had a fight with the owner of the rubber camp. Out there, in my camp among the rubber trees, I left behind hens, a dog, rice, pots, dishes; there were seventy sacks of Brazil nuts.[29] I said to a lady from Abancay, "Go to my camp, take everything that's there."

I guess the woman took my things. Who knows? I haven't gone back since. I came here, leaving everything behind. I had gotten into an argument with the owner. You know what happened? In January, I came to Puerto Maldonado and the owner gave all the things I had there to another rubber tapper. Damn, I didn't like that. I got back there and my things weren't there, damnit. So I asked the landlord.

"I've given them to so-and-so," he says. Shoot!

"So, Don Manuel, if I have a wife and I leave her at my camp? Do you give her a husband?!" I said to him, damnit.

---

27. Don Ignacio's other regional colleague and occasional rival, the late Edinson Panduro was a well-regarded healer based out of Puerto Maldonado, who considered Don Ignacio as one of his teachers and continued to visit and occasionally consult with Don Ignacio about patients until Panduro's death, several years before Don Ignacio's.

28. *Amarres* or "ties" are binding spells, loosely synonymous with *pusanga* or love magic, in which a person is "tied" to another, regardless of their will.

29. Don Ignacio uses the words *barricas de castaña*, meaning large bags of Brazil nuts. The Amazonian nut or Brazil nut is the nutrient-dense seed of the emergent tree species *Bertholletia excelsa* (Lecythidaceae). Brazil nut can rightly be understood as an ecological and economic keystone species and its harvest is one of the relatively few regional economies rooted in forest conservation rather than destructive extraction. The measuring unit used in the collection and commercialization of Brazil nuts, a *barrica* is a sack that contains between 65 and 80 kg of the seeds.

He didn't like that. I said all kinds of things to the landlord. Idiot, damnit.

"I don't want anything more to do with your rubber work. I'm leaving," I told him.

I went to my camp and got ready to leave in two days. I had half a hectare of cassava[30] planted, a beautiful cassava patch it was! Big, thick cassavas. I came here leaving it all behind; I never went back again. I brought two shotguns with me. Within three days I reached La Cachuela[31] and I stayed there for two days. I left in the afternoon and I got to my mother's house at night. I arrived at one in the morning.

I had a girlfriend. She was the reason I went to tap rubber. She gave me a grace period of four years to come back. Alright then, I disappeared for four years to the rubber camp, but she would always send me shotgun shells; she would send me all sorts of things. After four years I came back. Shoot, I say; I ask my mother about her. María was the girl's name.

"What about María, mom?"

"She's right there, in her house." she says.

"Tomorrow I'm going to go and see her."

"Go on then," she says.

That night I smoked my pipe and dang, in my dream I saw just how she was going to speak to me. The next day I went to see her, at eight in the morning after breakfast I went over there. Her cousin Antonio León, he says to me, "Hey, Duri, María is alone now."

Her parents had gone up the La Torre River.[32]

"They went hunting to the La Torre. Go and see her."

Following his advice, I went over there. In those days, well, there were very few people here. It was quiet around here in those days.

---

30. The edible roots of *Manihot esculenta* (Euphorbiaceae), an important Amazonian crop known in Peru as yuca.
31. Area close to the city of Puerto Maldonado.
32. La Torre River, located 60 kilometers from the city of Puerto Maldonado.

As I say, I smoked my pipe and had seen just what she was going to say. I got there and she was sweeping her patio. I said hello and we leaned against the fence. She didn't even say, "Let's go inside, let's sit down". I was there from about eight thirty until eleven in the morning, trying to win her over with words, as they say. You think she gave in? She just came out with buts. She was pregnant by another man, one Luca Silva. That's where it all ended. Well, I said goodbye. She has since passed away. I've had five girlfriends, including the mother of my children, and all of them are no longer living. I would have been a widower any way you slice it.

After I came back from Manuripi, they threw out the rubber tappers there. Well, it was Bolivian territory. They got rid of the Peruvians; they made them clear the rubber camp. That's when I came to Puerto Maldonado.

I lived in La Joya,[33] by where that bridge is now that needs to be filled in; down there is where we lived. My stepfather had bought it; yep, he had seventy hectares of property. In those days a hectare cost one sol. That's when he decided to buy it, the old man. He had one legitimate child. Francisco was his name, I mean, is his name. He sold the land, and once he sold the land, I came here, to Infierno. Now that idiot is wandering around like a fool, like a vagabond, because he didn't keep the land down there, damnit. It was close to the city too, seventy hectares, damnit!

---

33. Area near the city of Puerto Maldonado.

Rubber, Shiringa (*Hevea brasiliensis*) →

TWO

The Community of Infierno and the 1960 Flood

arrived to Infierno[34] in 1960. Since then, I haven't moved anywhere else. I was already with the mother of my children in those days. My daughter, the one that's in Lima, was the only one who had been born by then. There were three of us including her.

The owner of the land was one Martín Takahashi. I worked with him; he was a good guy, the Japanese man. He died in Lima; he had children too. There were lots of Japanese people here,[35] but they've all passed away by now. His Brazil nut camp[36] was in this area; I worked with him in those days. When people started to settle near here, I said to him:

---

34. The Native Community of Infierno was founded at a location already bearing that name (for disputed and ultimately unknown reasons). Located 19 kilometers from the city of Puerto Maldonado, province of Tambopata, department of Madre de Dios, Perú, along the banks of the Tambopata River. Officially recognized as a native community of the Ese'Eja ethnicity, Infierno is home to mestizos and people of various ethnic origins, even dating back to its founding—as evidenced by the presence of Ignacio himself, a Bolivian *ribereño*, or a native Amazonian not raised within the context of a specific ethnic group.

35. Famously and peculiarly, the Madre de Dios region became home to a significant population of Japanese immigrants, who reportedly were deserters escaping World War II.

36. This "camp" or *castañal* is an area of forest that naturally possesses a fairly high density of Brazil nut trees, worked by nut gatherers in a fasion not unlike the way rubber production forests are managed.

"What if I clear a farm patch at your camp?"

"Go for it!" he said.

That's why I cleared here,[37] see. I cleared a patch over there past the beach; I cleared the patch right in front of here. I opened one where Miguel Pesha lives now. Over here on this slope, there was an old trail which people used to walk down. Who made it? Probably the indigenous. In this whole sector there are old clay pots.[38]

We worked Brazil nuts with Don Eleodoro in 1960; he has also since passed away. I worked with him harvesting Brazil nuts here. We would harvest three hundred sacks! I don't know what ruined the Brazil nuts' production. Three hundred bags is how much that sector used to produce, but now I think it's not even a hundred. As if they were cursed, all the Brazil-nut trees dried up or were felled.

The village was going to be built over there at the point above the boat landing, there on that bluff. We requested the school for the community, Ricardo Nuñez, me and a guy from the highlands. There were three of us. We made the request for the school between the three of us; we went there to the local education authority. And on April 2nd –bam!– the teacher arrived. There was no school, nothing at all, really. At the campsite where we dried Brazil nuts, we set up a makeshift school.

There were seventeen students. My son Sixto joined the other students at four years old. That's why he finished primary school at age eleven. And the year when the school opened, my son Luchín was born. The teacher was his godfather; he tended to my wife when she was giving birth. I was away in town. We were going to come down to the community but I didn't come, and that night he was born. Julio Díaz was his name. He was young;

---

37. What is being opened or cleared (Ignacio uses the word *abrir*) is a patch of forest, in order to make a farm. Essentially all Amazonian farming begins with the clearing of a patch of forest.

38. Don Ignacio in fact dug up several potsherds and a couple stone axe heads when in the process of digging a latrine hole behind the house where he conducted ceremonies.

he was my *compadre*.[39] He left for Lima. I wonder where he's living now?

There were about seven families when the community was founded. These natives[40] were up there where the lodge is now;[41] there was a big beach there and that's where they lived. And when Velasco became president, indigenous communities were recognized and since these natives were here, done, this is now a native community.[42] That's when they tricked us, telling us that it would be easy to get loans from the bank, and the native community was founded. I still haven't seen any type of support from the State, up to this day.

In 1960, the flood happened. Man, it covered everything. It rained for eight days non-stop. It covered my little house; the rain toppled the house. It had knocked over a large lupuna[43] on the riverbank; the river swell lifted it up and threw the lupuna on top of the house, and this knocked the house over. It pushed it over there to the edge of the farm patch; the house was completely turned upside down. The house floated, since it was all very well nailed together, made with *crisneja*;[44] my little house, well it was brand-new.

I had two little dogs that used to go out hunting with me. Who knows how the little dogs managed to survive! After the flood died down and the river level resided, I came down to see them. The bitch was digging and the male dog had froth coming

---

39. Godfather of Ignacio's son. The *compadre* relationship is multifaceted but essentially one of mutual respect and support.

40. Ese'Eja people, the original inhabitants of the area straddling the present border of Peru and Bolivia.

41. "The lodge" is Posada Amazonas, an eco-tourist lodge joint-owned by the community and a private company and located within the native community's roughly 10,000-hectare territory.

42. Law of Native Communities and Agrarian Development of the Rainforest DL 20653, enacted during Juan Velasco Alvarado's military government. Decree-law by which the Peruvian State recognized the legal existence and legal personhood of native communities.

43. Tree known in English as the giant kapok, *Ceiba pentandra* (Malvaceae).

44. Panels of thatch woven from the leaves of *Geonoma* sp. (Arecaceae), a species of dwarf palm prized for durable roofing.

out of his mouth. Seemed like he was dying from hunger, right? There was a trunk of a manchinga[45] tree, that's probably how the dogs survived, it had their paw prints on it. They came down from there wanting to eat the hens that were buried in the mud.

In the branch of a tree, I found a partridge perched there, about to die too. Right there, I clubbed it, killed it and took it down. I found the dogs and put them on the canoe and went to see a certain Juan Vivantes, who was the uncle of the mother of my children. I went to see them. They were also just coming back from deep in the forest. They were there lighting their fire; everything was all covered in mud, you know. That's where I roasted the little partridge; I cut it into pieces and I gave half to the bitch and the other half to the male dog. I brought them back here again and they died from old age here. They were such good paca hunters![46]

---

45. Tree known in Central America as ramón or maya nut. *Brosimum alicastrum* (Moraceae).
46. *Picureros* is the word used to refer to dogs specialized in hunting the lowland paca, *Cuniculus paca*, or picuro, a large rodent with delicious meat, in Perú also known as majás. During the hunting sessions, dogs are used to facilitate the search and enclosing of the prey, or *mitayo*. That's why these dogs are referred to as *mitayeros* or *picureros*.

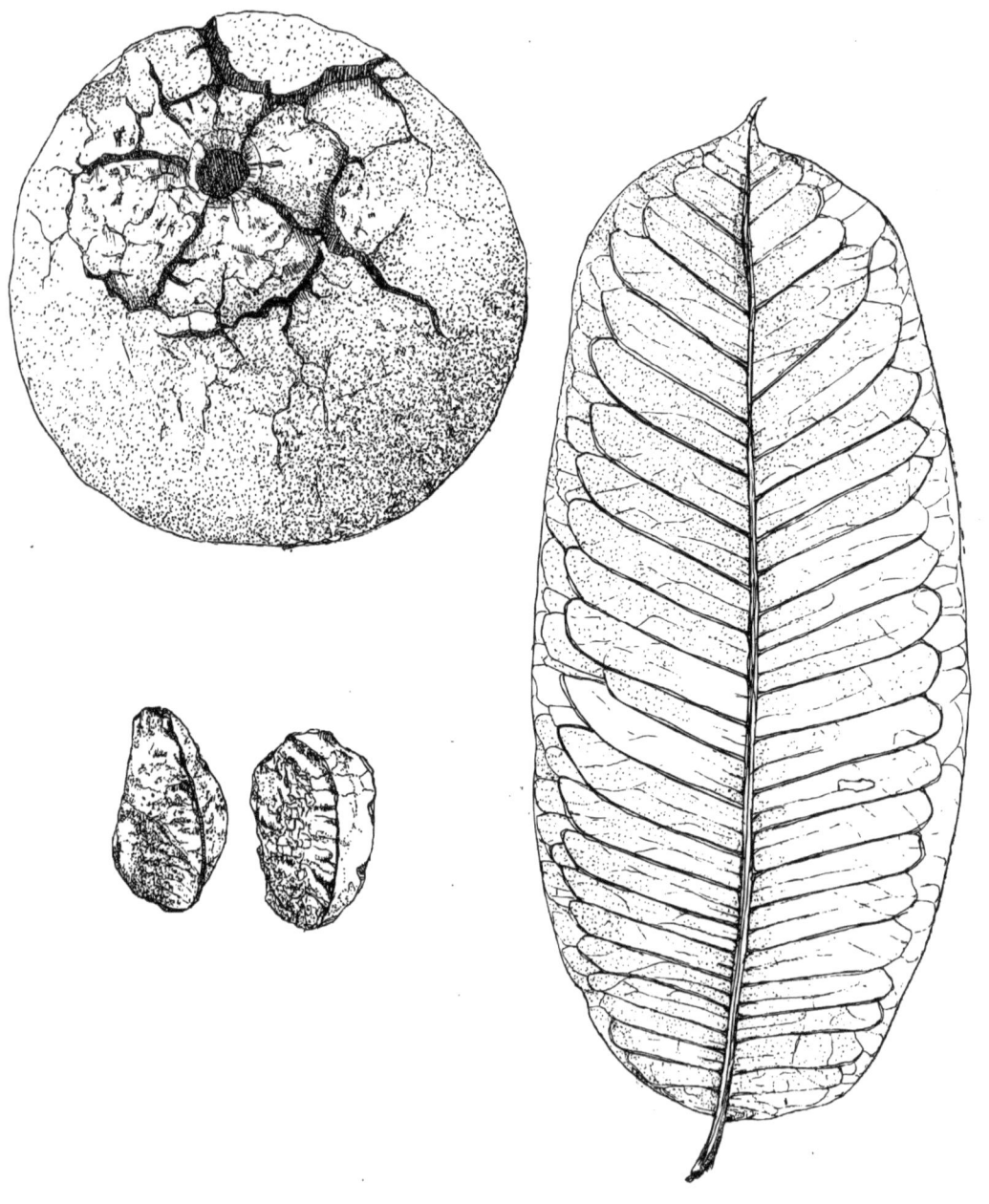

THREE

Getting to Know the Plant: A Ceremony in the Jungle

Seven times I drank ayahuasca with *maestros*.[47] On the eighth time, that old man who had been serving me, he told me, "You can drink on your own now; you've drunk seven times."

First I drank with Enrique Pacaya—he was from Pucallpa[48]— the old man was good people. He was tall and thin. Then I drank with Ricardo Caipo, a guy from around here, died years ago now. He was a con artist too, killed people, others have done *la contra** to him. Being bad doesn't work out. And Crisóstomo Prada—he was from Abancay—I also drank with him another time.

When you drink on your own it wipes you out! As I say, the first time I drank after the seven times I drank with maestros, I drank by myself in my house. It almost made me run away that night!

I had been learning this while I was working rubber; four years is how long I was tucked back out there. In my patch of forest, I

---

47. Teachers, masters. In the context of Amazonian herbalism, a *maestro* or *maestra* is a skilled adept at the healing arts, held in high esteem.
48. Previously Ignacio gave Pacaya's origin as Iquitos. In other conversations, the elder ayahuasquero's origin was stated as "Loreto." In any event, Pacaya was clearly from points north of Madre de Dios.

← Brazil Nut (*Bertholletia excelsa*)

*La Contra

The concept of *la contra* is used to describe a harmful spiritual response, such as from one shaman to another in a situation of antagonism. Rivalries between healers are very common in traditional contexts. Sometimes these conflicts are linked to the treatment of patients, such as, for example, the intervention by one shaman in the healing of someone harmed by the enchantment or curse of another shaman. Other times are simply cases of personal differences carried over onto magical planes.

La contra in its most pernicious form is intentionally unleashed with the aim of weakening the opponent's powers with disease or death by "harm" or sorcery. This type of attack is usually perceived by the targeted healer during his/her ceremonial work. The adversary attempts to disrupt the recipient's ceremonial and healing work, for example by obstructing the opponent's spiritual vision or healing chants, or other tricks meant to weaken a healer's spiritual prowess.

Don Ignacio sometimes remarked that when someone with a strong spirit is attacked, regardless of one's conscious intention or desire to not harm the attacker in return, one's guardian spirits could respond without waiting to be called to action. In such a case, la contra is not really an attack, but rather a sort of explosive spiritual self-defense with a will of its own.

Additionally, as previously mentioned, plants can sometimes lash out with their own contra, such as toward healers who are being negligent with their diets.

---

knew where ayahuasca grew; I recognized the chacruna.[49] I knew it all. One day, it was raining and I had brought in some ayahuasca. I got to cooking it, all day long. In the end very little came out. It was sweet, almost like honey! I drank a little bit of it, right? Then I waited but the dizziness didn't come on. I grabbed the rest of it that was left over and drank it. Five minutes later there's a sound behind my house: *peeeep, peeeeep!* The drunkenness, how strong it came over me!

---

49. Bush. *Psychotria viridis* (Rubiaceae). Plant with which the liana *Banisteripsis caapi* is complemented, resulting in the brew called ayahuasca. Chacruna is vital in order to access vision in the ceremony.

Darn it, I was in my bed; I had blocked the door to my room properly. When the drunkenness came over me strong, strong, then I was seeing crocodiles,[50] jaguars, all types of snakes; I saw animals I didn't recognize. They were huge, the jaguars, and they were running past me from one side to the other, dang it. I wanted to grab my shotgun to blow them away. I wanted to grab my axe to go and tap the milk of the rubber tree; I wanted to go into the jungle right there and then, you know? And then I realized that I had taken ayahuasca, damnit; that's when I came to my senses.

"I've taken ayahuasca. Ayahuasca is making me see," I said to myself.

I went out to the chicken coop; I had hens there. A snake had gone into my chicken coop and had swallowed a chick. I killed the snake. I'm coming back to my room and another fucker is right there. It escaped being killed by me. I entered my room and I kept seeing snakes. They wanted to come; they wanted to scare me, you know.

Man, it was raining, and since there was a roof gutter made of pona,[51] I got naked and bathed. I was on my own, you know. So I'm bathing myself, I'm there for about 10 minutes I guess, and the effects subsided a bit. Then I got out, went into my room and dried myself. I sat down and grabbed a cigarette. Geeze, I say, this isn't going to beat me. Then a voice says to me, "So you're a man, then."

If it hadn't been for that, it would have made me run off into the woods. Drinking by yourself is tough.

From there, I continued on my own; it no longer affects me quite as much anymore, even to this day. But now I'm tired of ayahuasca; I don't want to continue, but I don't have anyone to replace me.

Sometimes I would drink Ayahuasca and wouldn't eat the entire day, but you get skinny and weak if you don't eat the whole day. I dieted for four years. Through dreams and drinking the plant one sees. Also it teaches you about the weather; you pray to space and it teaches you. That's why I understand about the weather too.

---

50. Don Ignacio sometimes refers to the Amazonian caimans as "crocodiles."
51. Palm tree, *Iriartea deltoidea* (Arecaceae). Its round trunk is cleared of its central pulp and used frequently as pipes and gutters.

Ajo Sacha
Mansoa alliacea (Bignoniaceae)

You bathe yourself with that one, you fight with anyone and, well, you'll win. You have to bathe yourself and go into the jungle in the morning, or bathe yourself with it in the jungle and dry yourself after that. You get home in the afternoon and then you wash off. Just a quick bath is fine, it has already penetrated into your body.

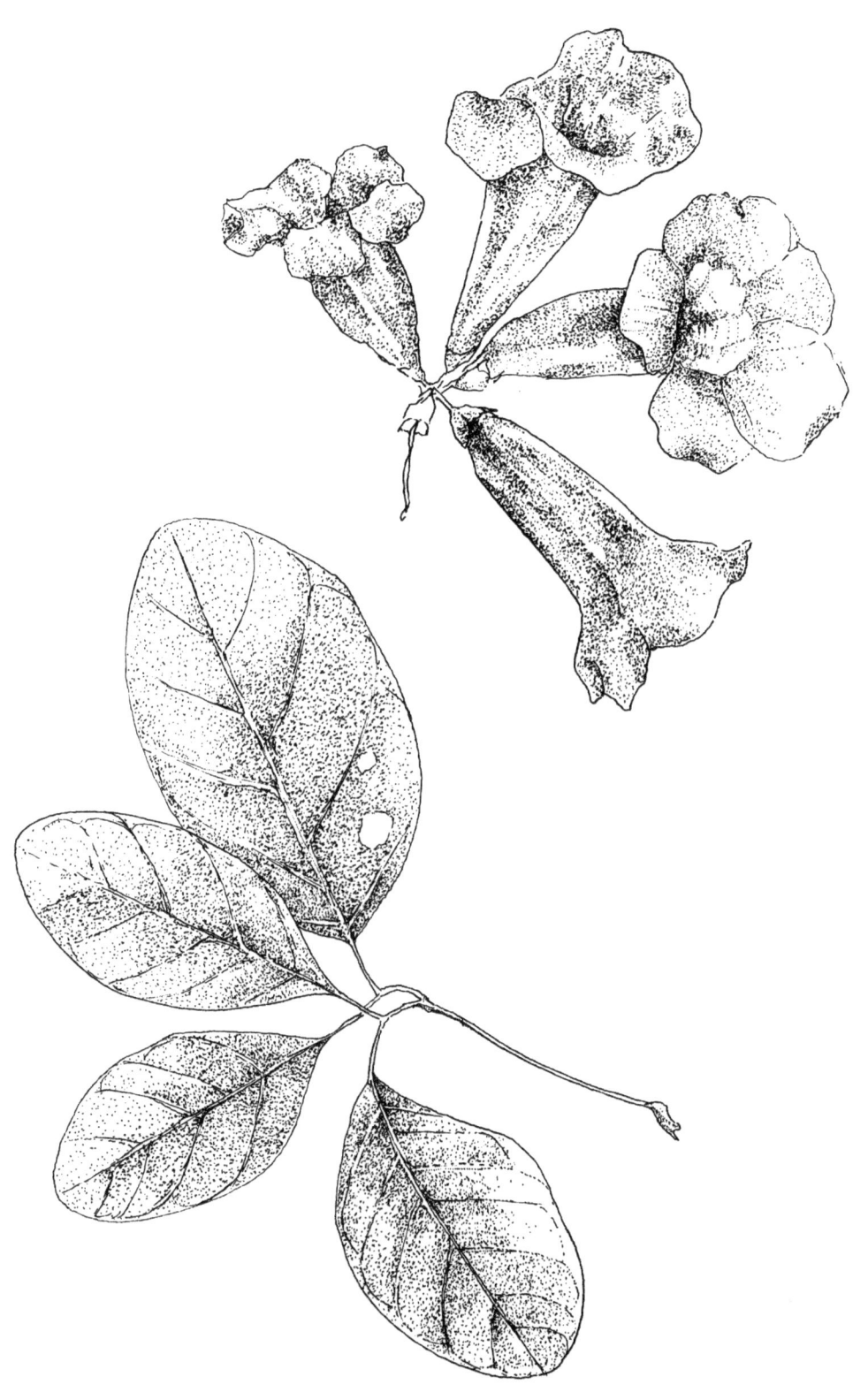

Arco Sacha
Hamelia patens (Rubiaceae)

This is for fungal infections. The leaf is boiled and with this hot water you rinse the place you have the fungal infection. That's the strength of this plant.

Ayahúma
Couroupita guianensis (Lecythidaceae)

The ayahúma is a tree similar to the Brazil nut.[52] *Right in the middle it bears its fruits, all around the trunk. This tree is bad and it is also good, just like ayahuasca. You take a strip the width of a finger, and four fingers long, that length of the shell of the fruit, and you cook it. You have to chop it up well and that's what you cook. If you want to be a good doctor, you diet for six months; you drink it like you would drink Ayahuasca. This one'll teach you well.*

---

52. The two species are botanical relatives from the same family, Lecythidaceae.

Azúcar Huayo
Hymenaea courbaril and *H. oblongifolia*
(Fabaceae)

Azúcar huayo works well prepared as a syrup to strengthen the blood. Its pounded bark is cooked just like ayahuasca, lots of it, more or less a kilo for each liter of syrup, and then you purify that like ayahuasca.[53] *The result is a tonic; you have to add sugar.*

It works to correct the blood, giving strength; you make people drink it for aches and pains. You take it like a tonic, every day, three times a day, only a teaspoon. It's a good syrup that one, for weak people.

---

53. With "purifying", Don Ignacio means the step in the cooking process in which the plant material is removed and the filtered brew is simmered down to concentrate it.

Barbasco
Tephrosia toxicaria (Fabaceae)

Barbasco is for itchiness all over the body, or as they say, the mange which dogs sometimes infect us with.[54]

To bathe yourself with the leaf, every new moon is when you bathe yourself with it, that's what it reveals to you. For baths against brujos[55] too.

To fish in the stream, you pound the liana, and it comes out white like milk. Little fish die very quickly; they're poisoned. That's why it's prohibited to poison the stream, because it kills the tiny ones too; it eliminates everything.

For uta,[56] its starch is extracted with a result similar to talcum powder. You wash the uta wound well, "dust" it with the powder and that's it.

---

54. Scabies.
55. Commonly translated as witch or witch doctor, *brujos* are malevolent shamans, equivalent in kind of knowledge and cultural stature, but dedicated to harm and personal gain, whereas the shaman should ostensibly be dedicated to healing and service, as Don Ignacio often stated.
56. The common name in Peru for leishmaniasis, a flesh-eating disease transmitted by flies in some parts of the Amazon basin.

FOUR

The First Ceremony
with Tourists

I was drinking ayahuasca, but I wasn't working with tourists yet. A group arrived here; there wasn't a road yet in those days. They got here in the afternoon; I don't know how they could have known that I drank.[57] That was in 1969, more or less around then.

So, well, this group arrived and they asked me. The guide was from Lima; Suárez was the guy's last name. He was quite the talker—the guy knew seven languages. Well, and he says to me, "And so, Maestro, do you take ayahuasca?"

"Yes, I used to, but not anymore."

"But you know it?"

"Sure."

The mixture[58] was right here.

"Shall we go find it?" he says.

"Alright, let's go then."

We found it, I cut it, we brought it down.[59] Since there were a bunch of them, fourteen of them, these Argentinians, well, one

---

57. *Tomo* in this context could be effectively translated as "I am someone who drinks." Ignacio often referred to ayahuasqueros or their students as "someone who drinks" or "one who takes," referring to ayahuasca but without saying it by name.

58. Ignacio often referred to chacruna as *la mezcla*, literally "the mix," with the accurate if technical-sounding term "admixture" providing the most proper translation. In any event, chacruna is called "the mixture" in the sense that it is mixed with ayahuasca.

59. As a woody liana, ayahuasca is found growing up into the crowns of canopy trees. Its harvest implies bringing it down (*bajar*) to be chopped to pieces on the ground.

brought in firewood, another one hauled in the water, others did the pounding.[60] We started at around this time of day, but it wasn't like how we boil it now; before you had to drink a whole mug. Not anymore. How could you drink one of those whole mugs? Drinking one of those nowadays would wipe you out.

Well then, we drank at around eight I guess; this was all jungle, young forest. Heck, they were drunk until the morning, all of them. I didn't know what it was to charge people at the time; they just gave me a tip. After that, in TPL—there's a lodge called TPL—they called me, and the manager tells me, "And how much do you charge?"

"Well, I don't know how much to charge," I tell him.

"No, you have to charge something. You tell us; you must charge something for your work."

From there, well, the others heard about me too. I used to go up and downriver, they took me all over. They were already paying me in dollars back then; they knew the price by then. I'm an idiot for not even owning a car... This plant keeps me in good shape, makes me too much of a kind person too. If not, gosh, I'd be a millionaire by now!

---

60. In Ignacio's preparation, ayahuaca vine pieces of roughly 40 cm in length were pounded with wooden clubs before being placed in pots with chacruna to cook.

FIVE

Apprenticeship: Curing with Sacha Bufeo[61]

That's the very first thing that ayahuasca teaches you... When I was learning in Manuripi, there was a lady. Her camp was over there somewhere; it was the one closest to mine. The lady had a daughter; she lived with that guy: Miguel, the guy was called. He had served in the army with me, and he lived with the lady's daughter. He had his campsite near where I used to tap rubber, and one day I go over there and the daughter says to me, "Don Ignacio, why don't you take my mother to your house?"

"You're taking me by surprise there, ma'am. I don't know her. I'd have to talk with her; we've never even spoken," I tell her.

"Well, 'cure'* her then!" she tells me.

"But I don't know how to cure," I tell her.

"How can you not know if you drink ayahuasca!" she says to me.

"Alright, fine, lady, but then whatever happens is not my responsibility, okay?"

"What do you need from her?"

"Take three hairs from the crown of her head."

The lady had grown her hair long. Before that, I was already learning about those plants. In Manuripi there are patches of

---

61. Epiphyte from the family Araceae without a confirmed botanical identification whose common name means "dolphin plant."

← Chacruna (*Psychotria viridis*)

> *** Curar (to cure)**
> The meaning of this concept within a shamanic context is twofold. On the one hand, "to cure" is understood as in the familiar usage, for example, to cure a sick person through the use of plants or prayer.
>
> On the other hand, to "cure" can be understood as seeking to attract someone romantically or sexually by casting a spell of sorts, with specific plants used for that purpose, or via enchantments.. The curing spells placed on a person in this context are known popularly as *pusangas*[62] or *amarres*.

these plants, you see. You go before breaking your fast, dang, you smell that fragrance; but if you go after having had breakfast, you don't notice a thing. I had some of the plant in my suitcase. You have to pick it while fasting and stow it away.

Later I went to Shiringayoc;[63] they had invited me to carnavales at my sister's. I'm walking by at something like two in the morning.

"Are you leaving already, Don Ignacio?" the lady asks me.

"Yes ma'am," I respond.

"Here's what you asked for."

She hands me a box of matches, I open the box and there's her mother's strands of hair, and since I had the plant in my suitcase, I put them there, I arranged them neatly, folded the leaf and put them in there. I left.

I spent three days at the carnavales and I returned on the fourth day; I got back at about four o'clock. Geeze, the lady, the mother, she was there shelling Brazil nuts.

"So, Don Ignacio, you're back now?" she tells me.

"Yes," I tell her.

"What did you bring me?"

"Nothing, you didn't ask me to bring you anything, ma'am."

---

62. In the Peruvian Amazon, *pusanga* is perhaps the most commonly used term for the broad category of love magic, potions, and spells.
63. Native community located in the province of Tahuamanu, department of Madre de Dios.

"You're so mean."

"Why?" Then I did give Doña Lourdes some crackers.

In those days the water crackers used to come in tins; I had bought like three kilos. I brought Vermouth with me, that drink still existed back then. It came in a large bottle, and I brought three of those and three more of alcohol tied up in a bag, three Vargas piscos.[64] Back then Vargas pisco was good.

And that afternoon the woman started to throw Brazil nut shells at me;[65] that's how it works when the person is under that plant, they start tossing whatever's lying around at you. Sheesh, I say, the lady is already worked over, and that's how it was.

That night we drank all night long. The second night the thing with the old lady was on. Gosh, damnit, eight days! I made the old lady get sick, she couldn't walk. I was young, see; I was twenty-three years old. But the woman didn't want to come with me. I wanted to bring her here to Puerto Maldonado and she didn't want to come.

Some time later, when I arrived here, there was a lady that lived further down that way, on the other side. I ran into her in Maldonado; she was kind of... Well, she'd had some beers. She says:

"So, Duri?" she says to me, "are you going home?"

"Yes."

"Let's go," she says, "I'm going home too."

The woman was chatting as we walked.

"Listen, Duri," she says, "I have a daughter, she married a teacher and I don't like that teacher guy. Why don't you grab her?" the lady says, right?

"But I don't know her, ma'am."

---

64. Pisco is an alcoholic distillate made from grapes, typical to the coastal valleys of southern Peru (where Pisco is the name of a city). Pisco Vargas is a brand from Ica, Peru.

65. Pieces of the empty shells covering individual Brazil nut seeds pile up around those doing the shelling. The shell pieces are small and lightweight, harmless if thrown at you.

"'Cure' her," she says.

"No, I don't know how to cure."

"How are you not gonna know if you drink ayahuasca?!" This lady says it to me that way too.

"But ma'am, I'm only just starting to learn."

"Let's go to my house," she says. "That's where she is."

"Alright then," I say to her, "but if you say so, not under my responsibility, okay?"

"Okay," she says.

To "cure" a girl, when you manage to catch her, you have to "heal" her yourself. You bathe her with herbs and then she's back to normal; because if you don't "heal" her she ends up kind of... kind of "popular". All these little things are there to be learned, if not she'll end up a bit mad from the herb. She could just attack you with a machete at any time; the girl ends up hating you. That's why you have to remove that thing from her yourself. But these dunces, what do they know? They don't know! I call them out. That's why I just watch them; when I work, I get to watching them.[66] You know why I'm saying this? Because it happened to me, when this lady told me to grab her daughter.

We got there at like one, two in the afternoon, I think. We went along chatting the whole way there, because it was still jungle in those days; there wasn't a road before.

We got to her house; the girl was there, her husband was in town. The girl doesn't pay any attention to me.

"I want to introduce you to a young man," the woman says.

She doesn't say anything, well she doesn't know me, see, and I don't know her either; it's the first time I've ever seen her. And the mother says to me, "What do you need from her?"

"Look, ma'am, if you say so... but taking no responsibility, like I said."

"Okay, don't worry about it," she says. "What do you need from her?"

---

66. To "watch them" (*mirar*) refers to visions within the context of Ayahuasca ceremonies.

"Alright, pull out three hairs from the crown of her head."

Then, at about five in the afternoon, her stepfather arrived.

"So Duri," he says, "you're out and about, eh?"

"Yes," I say to him.

What could his wife have told him, I think to myself.

"Ma'am, I'm off now," I tell her.

I didn't live far away either, it was right next door. I go to say goodbye.

"When will you come back?" she says.

"I'm coming back such-and-such a day ma'am; I'll come back again soon," I say to her.

And it's true, I even came back early on the day I had said. So the girl was walking behind me and her mother with her husband went ahead of me, and the girl was throwing dirt at me as she walked. I didn't say anything to her. Afterward, we went for lunch; we were together until two in the afternoon.

"I'm going into town, Elvira," her husband says to her. Elvira was his lady's name.

"Alright."

How did it happen? I guess he had talked to his wife about it beforehand. He went to bring two bottles of Cartavio, a rum they had in those days, two liters of that beverage. He came back at about five in the afternoon, bringing the booze.

"I'm off now, Don Jorge, ma'am," I told them.

"No, no," they said, "you're just getting started."

So I waited.

After a light dinner he brought out the liquor, the Cartavio rum. Shot after shot after shot, we finished first one and then the other. It was eleven in the evening by then.

"I'm off now, Don Jorge," I said to him.

"No! What a dummy. You're leaving already? This is your wife," he says, "Go on, Margarita, make the bed, for you two to sleep there."

I was drunk.

Early in the morning I wake up.

"Geeze, where am I?" I say to myself. It's not until then that I got with the girl. I woke up feeling hungry.

"Alright ma'am, I'm leaving now."

"Okay, when are you coming back?"

"Any day now."

"Okay, this is your house, that's your woman."

It was a done deal.

I was with her for a year and a month. After a year, I made some joke and she chased after me with a machete! She made me run around the house twice. That's when I stopped beside the path and I said to her, "Margarita, this is where our story ends. I can't trust you anymore; we're in a bad place," I said to her. "You follow your path and I'll follow mine," I said to her.

I didn't even say goodbye.

My canoe was at the boat landing. She ferried me across the river and I left. I didn't talk to her. She left me in a bad way. She attacked me. I didn't say bye or anything.

Do you know what happened? What had happened for her to get so angry as to attack me? She had said, "Look at my back."

Because she was fat, a crack formed between her buttocks. And I don't know why it occurred to me to spit there, but the spit ran down the crack of her ass and, well, she didn't like that. She shouted a bunch of nonsense and then chased after me with her machete.

I came over to my mom's place; she lived on the other side of the river, two kilometers inland.

I saw her one day, this woman, about a year ago, so old, so old, after many years. She lives by the Madre de Dios. Thin, tall, gray-haired, as old as it gets, but she's younger than me.

Back then, I still didn't know the process of the plant. That's why one who knows, one who uses these plants, has to learn it all. At that point I ran into a man called Noé, from la Cachuela. That man was a technician, a smalltime brujo, and I told him about it.

"You're such an idiot!" he says, "you have to heal her yourself."

That's what the little old man told me. It turns out that when you cure her with the plant and then you're with the woman, you have to bathe her with other plants so she becomes normal again, with her own affection now, not from the remedy anymore, that doesn't remain. And they don't know that around here; it's just difficult to learn that.

SIX

La Contra for Sacha Bufeo: Tongoy Sacha[67]

All plants must be sought out while fasting; that's when you'll recognize them. The leaf must be picked while fasting and the person's hairs must be rolled up inside. You take it, fold it up and put it in your bed. For three days you don't have any "interviews" with the person at all. On the fourth day you just look at him or her; if they talk to you, answer, but don't pay them too much attention. The second time you see them, then you do talk to them. The process of this plant is to cure the person, and once they are with you, you have to heal them with other herbs. There are herbs to counteract this herb: it's called tongoy sacha. This has a very straight stalk and its fruit is a bit longish, like a passionfruit. That plant is very powerful. You bathe the person with the tongoy sacha itself. Trick the person by telling them it'll bring them good luck; that's what you tell them, because if you don't cure them they'll stay sort of airheaded, sort of…"popular". But you yourself have to do it because that plant is very strong, you see. I have faith in it; I've cured several women.

This plant is for curing girls or anyone that has been worked over with plants. There are two words used to describe that: "potion;" and it's also called *pusanga*.

---

67. A shrub or small tree from the genus Vasconcellea, in the family Caricaraceae.

← Tongoy Sacha (*Vasconcellea* sp.)

My ball and chain's sister, Manuel's son worked her over with some herbs; I think it was with sacha bufeo. Shoot, the girl went crazy! She despised everyone, wanted to go far away; they said she wanted to go to town to work.

One day I'm walking past on the way to my farm patch and she's sitting there in her doorway; I knew the girl, you know.

"And, Florcita, what's up with you?" I say to her. She looked sad, you see.

"Nothing!"

"What do you mean, nothing? You're in a bad way. Let me know what's going on," I tell her.

"There's nothing wrong with me."

"You're not okay. Let me know so I can bring you herbs to bathe with."

"No, there's nothing wrong."

I went to my farm, I left. The next day, her mother says to me:

"Don Ignacio, don't you know plants? This is what's happening to Flor, she's been worked over with a plant remedy."

"Yes ma'am, I just saw her and she told me nothing's wrong. But she's not okay," I told her.

"Yes, she's not okay. She hates everything; she loathes us. She had an argument with her sister. Her sister started crying. That's the state she's in. Do you know of a remedy?"

"Sure I do! I'm telling you that I met with her in order to bring her the herb."

"She's crazy, she wants to be over there where that boy is. Bring me the plant then."

And I brought her the plant. But she didn't want to bathe with the plant, you see. So I said to her mother:

"Ma'am, this is what you're going to do. You're going to crush the leaf of this herb a little bit and soak her clothes in that. Dry them in the shade and in the afternoon, you make her bathe."

When her clothes had the plant on them, she said to her:

"Your clothes are right over there."

And the following day she woke up much better already. Then she came to her senses.

"I was in a bad way; they cured me… That bastard," is what she had said.

She said her head was exploding. That headache made her cut her hair herself.

Then the old lady says to her, "You see? You don't want to bathe with those plants. Don Ignacio told me to soak your clothes with them and that's what I made you wear and you're fine now."

"Alright, have him bring the plant then."

Since I know several of the plants, I took it to her. One single bath was enough! That's one kick-ass plant to counteract pusanga. She starts hating him; if she can, she'll attack him with a machete! Sheesh, but incorrectly applied, you see. They don't know how to do those things, because it's not supposed to put the woman in such a state. And now she hates the boy.

One time there was this other guy; we were coming from Maldonado. There didn't use to be a road. We came together by motor boat. That guy always used herbs to get women. The guy grabbed that plant (sacha bufeo), but he didn't diet at all, you know? He would go to the port in town and work the women with herbs; and that plant is very jealous too, you see, but you have to keep its diet, right? You shouldn't abuse the plants too much.

We're heading upriver; we were coming back from a trip to town.

"There's something wrong with me, damnit, and I don't know what it is," he tells me.

"What is it then?" I say to him.

"I'm in a bad way. I don't have any money; my kids don't listen to me—they've abandoned me. I can't do anything about it; they've even sold one of my plots of land. I'm alone now, I don't have anyone to look into it for me," he says. "Can you suss out what ails me?"

"Let's see, show me your hands then," I tell him.

He shows me his hands and they were all knobby looking, see. That plant was hurting him. I looked him over thoroughly.

"What a dummy you are," I told him. "Why do you get involved with things you don't know anything about?" I immediately recognized it in him. "To get involved with that, you have to know what you're doing; you can't just use the plants just like that," I told him.

And he says to me:

"How about if I go to your house for you to heal me?"

"Come on over then."

And he never arrived.

That plant kills you if you don't know how to use it, for using the herbs without following a diet. That plant is harmful to humans too. If you don't follow the rules, it'll carry you off too. Everything has its process.

Jergón Sacha rhizome (*Dracontium* sp.) →

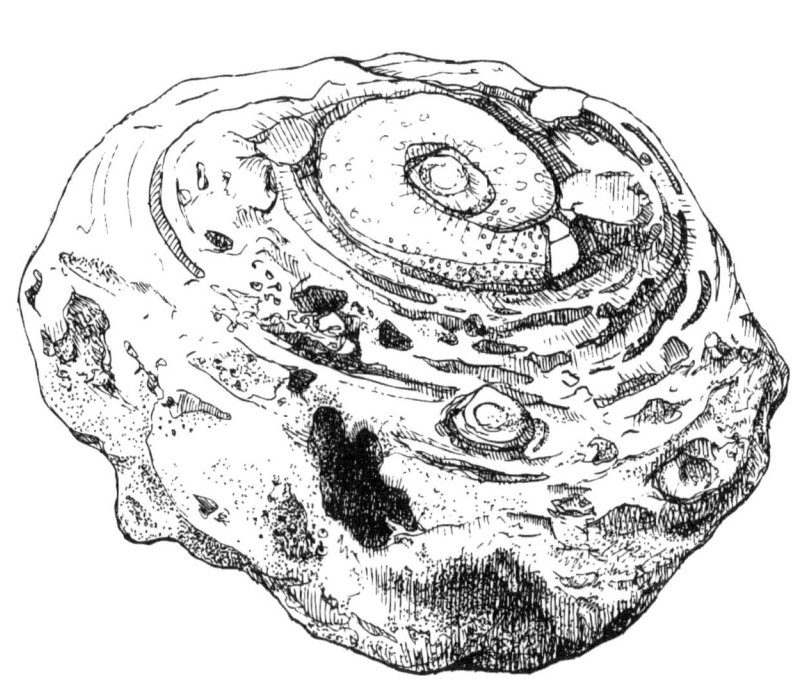

Bijahuillo
Heliconia sp. (Heliconiaceae)

This is good to treat ringworm. Pounded, its slimy liquid is stuck on the affected area.

Brazil Nut, Castaña
Bertholletia excelsa (Lecythidaceae)

The resin from the Brazil nut tree is for itchy skin—either the resin or, just as good, the boiled bark to wash yourself with. Some also drink the Brazil nut resin. They leave that resin rolled up with tobacco in a place where nobody goes and at six in the evening you go there and it will have become viscous, like a phlegm. You swallow that. You're going to keep its diet. After a month you give it a try; you cough up a bit of phlegm and that's used to cure.[68] Here nobody knows that. As I say, we know now, we say we know, but we don't know anything. We only know a little bit about just a small number of herbs.

---

68. This magical sounding "healing phlegm" is known in some parts of the Amazon as *madidi*. On other occasions Don Ignacio described having seen one of his teachers produce from his mouth and then use the phlegm in a healing, only to later swallow the phlegm again once the treatment was concluded.

Caña Caña
Costus sp. (Costaceae)

This is good for treating internal fever.[69] Boil its tuber and drink a cup of the boiled liquid and have a normal bath, as hot as you can tolerate, and immediately go to bed, all wrapped up in blankets.

---

69. *Fiebre interior* as Don Ignacio calls it, is a kind of gastro-intestinal infection producing heat in the body.

Capirona
Calycophyllum spruceanum (Rubiaceae)

Scrape the bark and mix it with a little bit of water; together with the liquid from the bark, rub it on the skin of anyone suffering from pimples.

Cashapona
Socratea exorrhiza (Arecaceae)

When you have nightmares, that's what that one is for. Look at that cashapona with all its branches, that's where you walk through. You walk in between its roots, going in straight and coming out to the left, walking around it just three times.[70] You'll never get nightmares or anything of the sort. This is a really nice secret. Someone came to me once complaining that they couldn't sleep; I took the person into the forest. I had dreamt it, you know, it taught me how to do this work in my dream and it worked out well; it works well.

---

70. Cashapona is known in English as the "walking palm," due to its tripod-like aerial root system and its supposed ability to slowly move across the forest floor by sending out new roots in one direction as the older roots decay. The base of the trunk of this palm is suspended above the ground by roots descending on all sides like the poles of a tipi. For this "secret," Don Ignacio recommends walking under and through the root system, which for many walking palms is well over a meter in height.

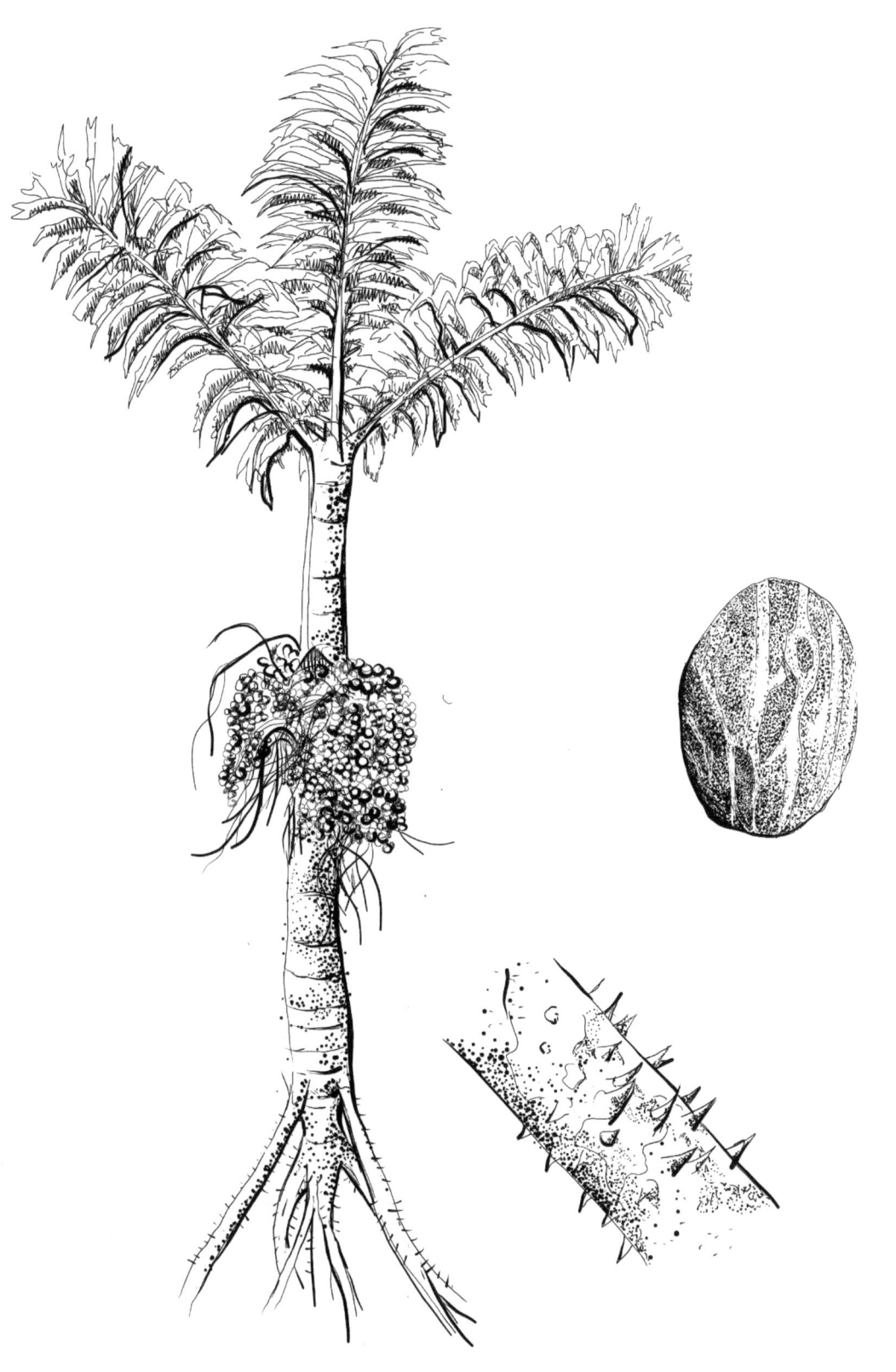

SEVEN

The Plant's Punishments

Once when I drank Ayahuasca, it made me ill. I drank it and I was dieting forty days, and the owners of the camp had killed a cow. I was hungry and, well, I ate some. I went back home and I was dieting the plant. I went back to my house and I had a little pain in my side. The next morning, I woke up and I couldn't stand up straight. I couldn't go into the forest or anything, nowhere; I was just lying in bed. That day, I spent the entire day in bed. Out there, where are you gonna go to ask for help?

The next day I was lying in my bed, and there was this guy that I'd been in the army with. Abel Tinari was his name. He was a loudmouth. My house was over here, let's say, and the path ran past right nearby, and just there was my rubber smoker where I cured my rubber. He walked up singing, whistling, and from over there he shouted at me.

"Amigo Duri!"

"Ah?" I say to him. "What's going on, Don Abel?" I shout to him from my bed. I was lying in bed, see.

"And Duri, my friend?" he comes up to my room, where I was. "What's up with you?" he says to me.

"Man, I'm a little sick," I tell him.

"What's wrong with you?"

"I don't know what I've got."

So he got to cooking. Damnit, I hadn't eaten a thing. There was meat in the kitchen, a bit of everything, there was always meat. There were lots of animals there! I always killed the best you

← Huayruro (*Ormosia* sp.)

could hope to kill around there. There were also lots of *otorongos*.[71] I had otorongos walking right through my patio.

My clothes were there; they had been soaking for three days on the washing board in the stream. He went and washed my clothes, left them drying out in the sun and then fed me.

"What do you want now?" he says to me.

"Look, Don Abel," I tell him, "I want you to do me a favor, if you can."

"What's that then?" he says to me.

"Could you call Prada and Caipo?"

"Sure!" he says.

It must have been around two in the afternoon. He grabbed his shotgun and went running off. It was pretty far from there to get to where the neighbors lived, like two and a half hours. He gets there and they say to him, "What's up, Don Abel?"

"I've come calling for you on behalf of my friend Duri. He's not well; he's bed-ridden."

"What's wrong with him?"

"I don't know what's wrong with him. He's asking you two to go and see him."

Caipo was there and he says, "Shoot, let's go and see him."

At that moment, they started to cook Ayahuasca, it was probably three, four in the afternoon. They arrived at like nine at night. I was there in my bed, groaning. The one from Abancay says to me, "So, Duri, my friend, what's wrong with you?"

"I don't know what's wrong with me, Don Crisóstomo."

He lifts up the mosquito net.

"Poor bastard," that's all he says to me. "You're a poor bastard."

Then Caipo, he knew more than the other one, lifts up the mosquito net and says to me, "Why'd you go getting too big for your britches?" he says to me.

"Dang, you're a coward, aren't you?" Prada says to me. "Fool, the plant is messing you up."

---

71. A name of Quechua origin for the Amazonian jaguar, *Panthera onca*. The animal is also known as "painted tiger" (*tigre pintado*) in the area.

They made me sit over there. They drank ayahuasca. They only gave me a little bit. At around eleven at night, they took me outside. There was a post stuck in the ground there where my clothesline was tied and right next to it there was a lemon tree. It wasn't big, the lemon tree, it was still small. *Oof,* I saw its little flowers, how they were falling down, very fragrant to me in that drunkenness I was in.

One of them was here and the other one over there; they were singing and they tell me, "You're going to go in circles right here around this post."

And there I was, running around. They were closing me in with tree trunks around me so the rivals wouldn't find me, hiding me out—one of ayahuasca's secrets, you know. Then they said, "It is done." They took me inside the house, both of them blew smoke over me,[72] and the next day I woke up feeling much better.

"You're going to diet for eight days, you dummy," they told me. And I got better.

The plant had done me harm. That's why I say that you have to have experience, you can't just use this plant just like that. Apparently, the tip of its *chonta*[73] was sticking into my heart. If it pierced it, it would have killed me. That's why I know about all this nonsense!

Ayahuasca is fucking tough. That's why I laugh at all these ayahuasqueros that say "Ah, but ayahuasca this and ayahuasca that…" Do you think they're going to fool me? I've had all sorts of situations with ayahuasca; it has made me soil myself completely with poop, and it's also made me urinate my bed.

---

72. *Soplar,* to blow on someone, meaning with tobacco smoke, is a form of treatment employed both in and outside of ayahuasca ceremonies, for certain illnesses considered to be spiritual in origin, such as an acute fright or scare. The skill of the healer is measurable by the effectiveness of these kinds of simple but powerful treatments, by his or her ability to perform clearing and heal with the breath in this way.

73. A *chonta* can be understood as the manifestation of the harmful power of a plant or spirit which materializes in a physical object similar to a thorn or an arrow tip. Chonta in a different context refers to the black palm timber of pijuayo, or *Bactris gasipaes,* used for making spears, lances, harpoons, and arrowheads. The chonta of a plant in this context could also be likened to a poison dart, a common Amazonian hunting weapon, referred to by Ignacio on other occasionas as *virotes* or *dardos*—darts.

One time, there were seven travelers. We worked with José from Loreto. We finished the ceremony at one, and at Volcán's place there was a carnavales celebration. That's where he went; I didn't want to go. I came up here to my house. I had gotten into bed, and he tells me, "No, *paisa*,[74] come with me!"

"No, paisa, I'm here now, the beer with the ayahuasca might make me fall over," I say to him.

"No, paisa," he says to me. "How can I go on my own? Come with me."

"Alright then, let's go," I told him.

We had finished at around one and the tourists paid us right there and then. They gave him, I don't know how many dollars; they gave me seven hundred.

Right away, damn it all, the guy from Loreto orders half a crate of beer. Then, to not be left behind, I order another half a crate, and from then on, I continued drinking. He cheated me out of my money, that guy from Loreto, that idiot… I didn't say anything to him.

We finished the beers and I tell him, "I'm off."

And I couldn't walk; I was already tanked from the beer and ayahuasca. I guess it was the belly full of beer! That's when they came to leave me here; Condori brought me back here, left me in my bed, I don't even remember.

That's when I peed myself. I woke up all covered in poop, damnit! Geeze, I get up early in the morning, sheesh, my cot stank; I realize I had done number two and peed all over too. Do you think I remember, though? Not a damn thing. That's why I say, "Why?" Well, that's called doing it to yourself, right?

The plant has also made me get lost several times around here, even though that might sound like a joke. And some say: "Oh no, it doesn't affect me at all." How is that? They just don't want to say anything, they don't want others to know what happens to

---

74. *Paisa* is short for *paisano* or compatriot, a term of affection for someone from one's country or region—which Ignacio often used to refer to other ayahuasqueros.

them. They don't let you see what their life is like; it's like they blind your eyesight. You can't see anything.

Ayahuasca has its rules. If you're a bad person, it will beat you up. But if you don't follow its rules, it'll slam you just the same way. Ayahuasca has two paths: for doin' good and for doin' bad. If you want to learn for bad, you'll learn all bad things, and if you want to learn as a healer it'll take you longer.

I don't know how to do harm to people.[75] I don't know why so many become bad; to do ill to people, right? I don't know how to do people harm; I don't understand what witchcraft is like. I do heal it; I treat those to whom harm has been done. Many sick people have come to see me. You have to have belief, someone from above, a power, you know. I worship Jesus Christ, San Antonio, the Virgin of Chapi, the Virgin Mary. They never allow you to do wrong.

It's easier to learn to be bad, the timeframe is shorter. To be good you have to diet more, about two, three years. Didn't I tell you I was tucked back deep in the forest for four years?

Women learn more quickly than men; they have more—what could it be?—a stronger spirit, more wisdom. History tells us, some say, that a woman beat out the devil. That must be why women are more powerful. It depends on the woman, of course; if she's really interested, she'll learn well, without a doubt.

Ayahuasca is a very "jealous" plant; well, its diet is very strict. The people that accompany you in your home can only be your family. When I married the mother of my children, I would drink it and not sleep with her. I slept in a different room and that's how it went.

The recommendation is that, in terms of food, you have to eat thin plantains and *fariña*.[76] And meats: pava[77] and deer.[78] If it's a large animal, collared peccary:[79] its front left leg and only if it's a female. Not just any type of meat, nor salt. Then, you have to eat

---

75. *Daño*, harm, in this context refers to a curse-like act of ill-will sorcery (*brujería*) that harms the recipient.
76. A bland dry cereal made of toasted cassava (*yuca*), a popular and easy-to-store dried food.
77. A rainforest bird appreciated for its meat. *Penelope jacquacu*.
78. Amazonian red brocket deer (*Mazama americana*), a much-prized game meat.
79. *Dicotyles tajacu*, a pig-like animal known in Peru as sajino.

those thin little plantains, rolled around in the coals, and the person roasting them, if the person is taking ayahuasca, they must turn them over with a long stick from afar and not get close to the fire.

Sometimes when you're on your diet, really concentrated, you go out and, *boom*: you run into a lady. Maybe that lady is on her time of the month; sheesh, that brings you crashing down! When you're keeping to your diet properly, you feel that, you feel all of those little things. This plant, ayahuasca, is very jealous then! People, they prepare it, they drink it, but they don't follow its real process. You have to diet it right. To be bad is easy to learn, it's faster than to become a healer; it's easier. When you're surrounded by people, it's not easy to learn; you learn, but only a little bit.

We were invited to a course, a workshop about ayahuasca. Someone came from Pucallpa, because Pucallpa is where many ayahuasqueros come from, right? A girl who was a botanist came from Lima, and there was a man who was a chemist, a Swedish guy who was a technician, and Doctor Cayetano. He was with us here for eight days. And that's when they asked us, right in this workshop, who drank ayahuasca. Since ayahuasca used to be illegal, you weren't supposed to drink it, you see. Don José's dad said, "Don Ignacio over here drinks ayahuasca."

So I got up.

"Yes, there are many of us who drink ayahuasca, but in secret because the police persecute us."

The guy stood up, the chemist.

"What do you mean, professor, is ayahuasca illegal?" he said to him.

That's when the one from Pucallpa got up.

"No, not anymore, you can now drink it anywhere and nothing will happen to you."

I also consider it to be a drug, but it teaches you, you learn from it, right? And you learn to recognize the good people, the bad people, it teaches you all that when you've kept to your diet.

Lime, Limón (*Citrus* X *aurantifolia*) →

EIGHT

Dreaming

It was in dreams that they wanted to make me sign a contract. A man dressed in white, but he was black, he came and he talked to me.

"You're going to sign a contract."

He put a table in front of me. There was something that looked like a heart, and a book of black writing for me to sign. I refused to sign and started to recite the Lord's Prayer, and the guy turned into a cat and *boom!* He ran off into another room. He tried three times. After the third time, he told me he was leaving.

"I'll come back for the second round," he said to me.

He never came back again.

That contract is no good, see; you'll be with Satan then. You're good and you're bad then. They wanted to do that but I didn't let them; I didn't agree to signing.

In another dream it was the same thing. Someone wanted to give me a guitar as a token, to teach me the songs, I guess, the ícaros, but I refused then too. Learning is nice, but you shouldn't take the wrong path, that's no good.

One other time I dreamed I was climbing a tree, a tall pijuayo tree.[80] I climbed high up the pijuayo, and when I got to the crown of the pijuayo, well, the pijuayo broke off and came falling down. I was falling, and I said the name of the Virgin of Chapi and I came to a stop in midair. From that moment on, I worship the

---

80. Palm tree. *Bactris gasipaes* (Arecaceae).

Virgin. If I hadn't called her name, I wouldn't be talking to you now. I guess someone put la contra on me, you see; that's how it is when they do la contra to you.

(…) Let me tell you a dream. There was a large plot of pasture-land and there were cattle there, and the cattle charge at me; they come chasing after me, darn it. I run to the barbed wire fence and *boom!* I throw myself over to the other side. I make it over the wire fence and I get to a stream; there was a little log to cross. On the other side, there was a little tree that had thin branches and a *huayo*[81] that's prickly; its fruit is yellow. I climbed up it and looked across the stream and it was no longer cattle but a man, some bastard, and he says to me:

"You're screwed now."

He caught up with me and starts up the tree, and I had my little harpoon, my little spear with me.

"And what are you here for?" he says to me. "Now you'll find out what's gonna happen to you."

"What's going to happen to me?" I say to him.

Right there I nailed him with the spear, *chooff*. I knocked him over and he fell down. In my dream I almost killed him; he was a bastard and it was him chasing me. Those bastards never came after me again.

That plant is actually really good. It's a tree in the forest that bears fruit; its fruit is small and yellow. The tree is thorny and has lots of branches. The plant you climb up is for your defense, see.

All plants with thorns are bad; the ones without thorns are good. A lady revealed to me in my dreams that I should bathe myself with that coconilla,[82] thorns and all, but that's to protect oneself. If they chase after you, you're in there surrounded by the thorns and they can't reach you. You just bathe yourself with its growth buds.

---

81. An idiom of the Peruvian Amazon, *huayo* means a fruit.
82. Herbaceous plant, *Solanum sessiliflorum* (Solanaceae).

There was another time when they chased me; I have dreamt of being chased my whole life. I had a small patch of sugar cane. I was clearing it. I was on my own. And there was a vine of ajo sacha;[83] I pulled it down and it fell in a pile at my feet. I grabbed a serving of it and came home. At six in the afternoon, I went to bathe myself with the plant and went straight to bed. That night I dreamed… shoot, I chased the bastards off by force. They didn't come after me again; but now they're after me once more.

When my son was learning, in a dream I saw him at the top of a lupuna tree in a lake. The lupuna was in the middle of the lake; he was at the top and I was down here. And he was grabbing the fruit and throwing it down at me from up there, and I was catching it in my dream. That's bad; you only grab hold of bad things, that's why he doesn't want to learn.[84]

---

83. Vine (liana), *Mansoa alliacea* (Bignoniaceae). Don Ignacio differentiates it (*ajosacha de soga*) from the tree ajosquiro, *Gallesia integrifolia* (Phytolaccaceae), which he calls *ajosacha de palo*.
84. In reference to shamanic learning.

Peach Palm, Pijuayo (*Bactris gasipaes*) →

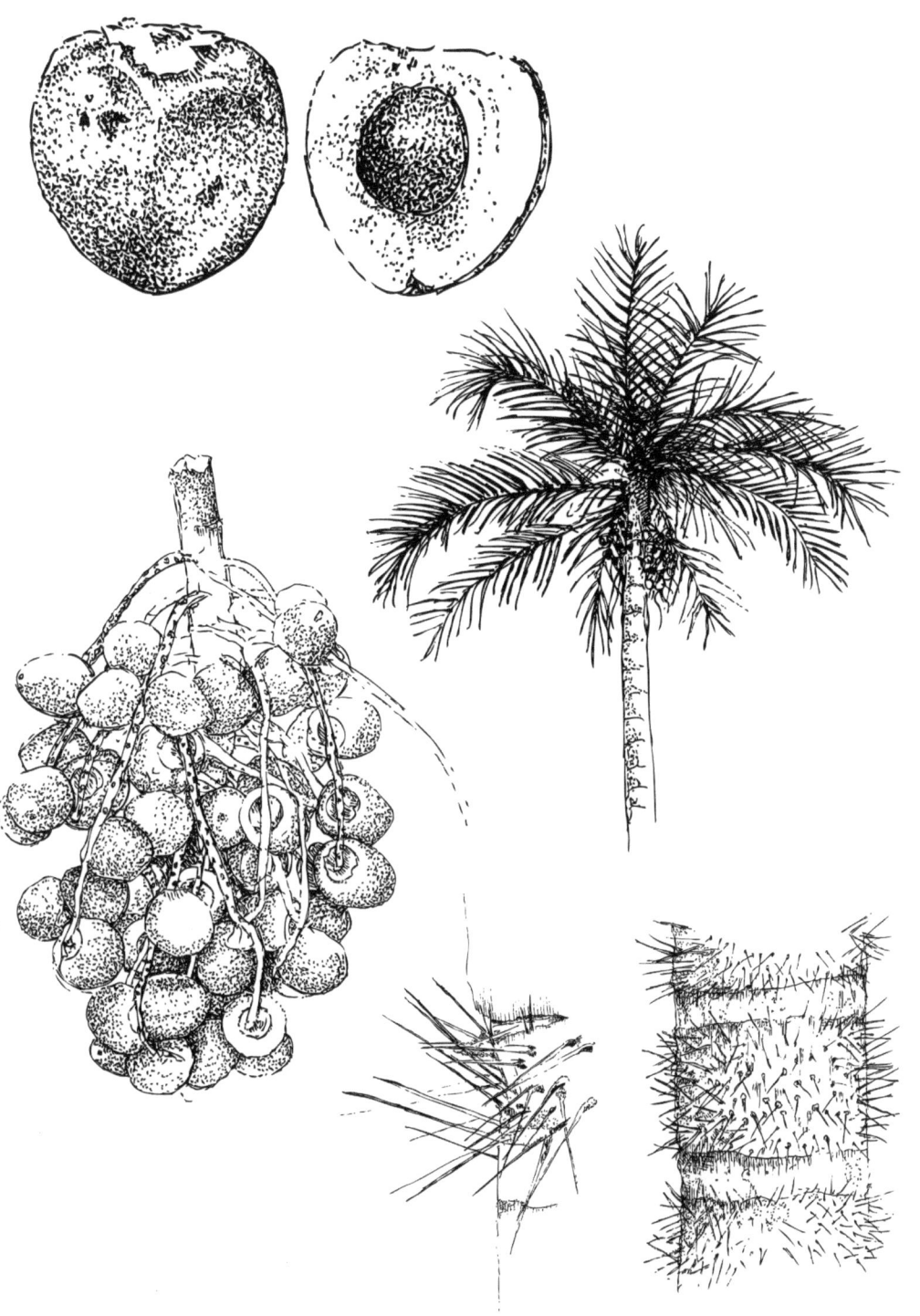

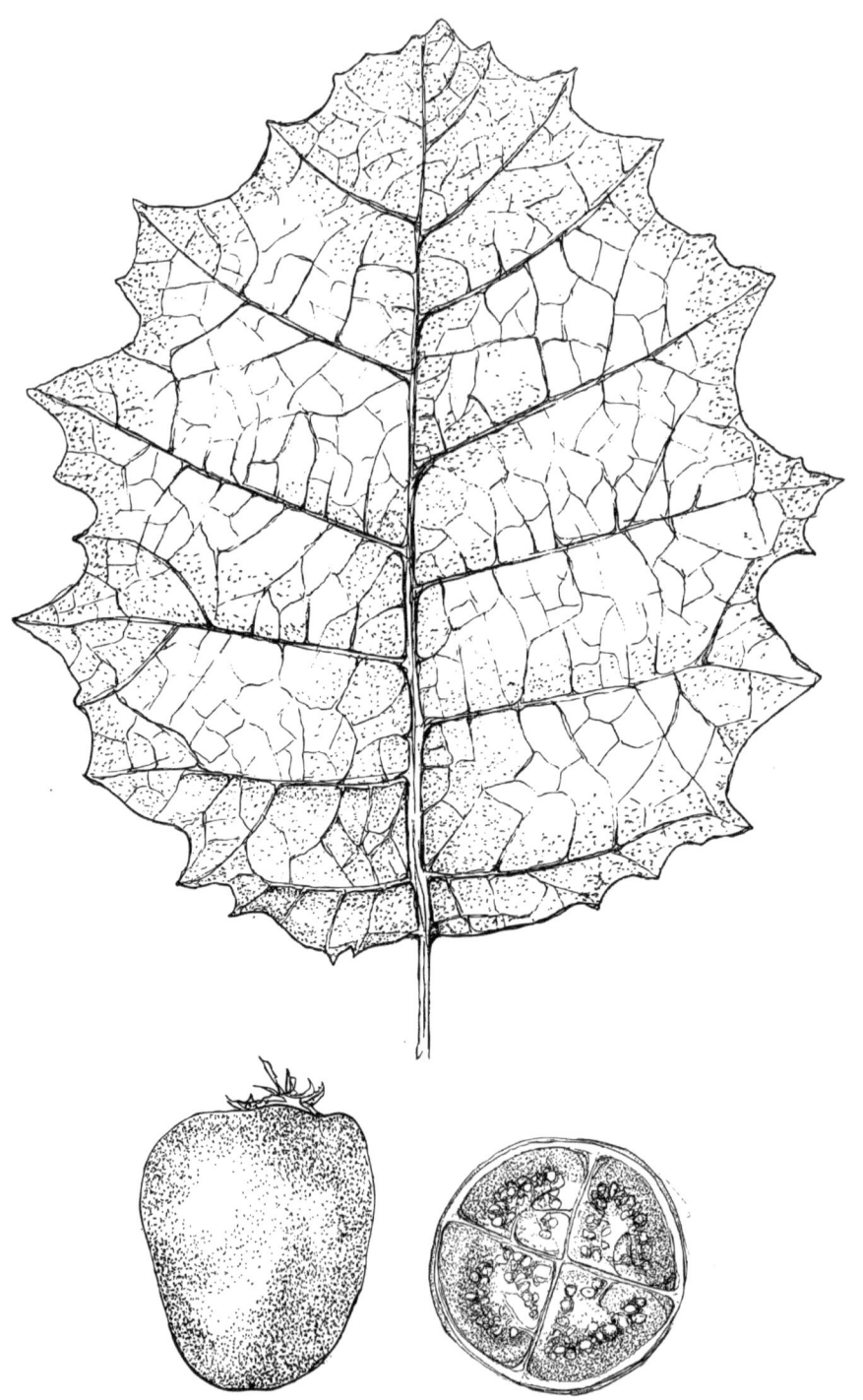

NINE

The War Between Tobacco and Ayahuasca

Learning from tobacco[85] is wonderful. I drank it, right, a big gulp of it,[86] to hell with it. I went inside my house. I was on my own! I was working rubber at the time. I took it twice. I'll tell you about the first time, when it made me dream.

It went like this: there were three musicians. One had a drum, the other had a violin and the other an accordion. So, according to the dream, they're playing, and the musician with the accordion pulls apart his accordion, he damages it. And the violinist too, the neck of his violin is all bent; and the drum player makes a big hole in his drum as he's playing. That's my dream. Then, a large, curvy lady appears, a nice lady, good-looking.

"You could use a bit more frankness."

That's what she said to me, I don't know why.

After that I drank again to see what it meant. With the ayahuasca, they get into a fight. The mother* of tobacco is a man with a big hat on and the mother of ayahuasca is a short man.

---

85. Plant. *Nicotiana rustica* and *N. tabacum*. (Solanaceae). Varieties of black tobacco from the Amazon, commonly known as *mapacho*.

86. He refers to ingestion of tobacco in liquid form, after soaking the leaves in water and extracting this liquid, consumed for ceremonial and learning purposes. It is also used as a purgative to cleanse the body and the gastrointestinal tract in particular.

← Coconilla (*Solanum sessiliflorum*)

*Madre

Under this conceptualization, the word "mother" can be understood as synonymous with the spirit of a plant, a river, a mountain, or of any element of nature to which magical, sacred, healing and/or protective characteristics are ascribed.

The mother of a plant is the plant's consciousness or the manifestation of its spirit as a personification of its being, which might be an animal, an insect, a person with certain physical characteristics, and so on. For example, the mother of the tree known in the Peruvian Amazon as tangarana (*Triplaris* sp., Polygonaceae) is the ant that lives inside it and shares its name. According to Don Ignacio's experience, the mother of the ungurahui palm (*Oenocarpus bataua*, Arecaceae) is a woman with long green hair, who revealed herself to him in a dream.

So in my dream, I was dreaming about nothing but girls. They were in a big stream, in a little river playing war games, splashing water at each other to see who would win. I'm on a bluff above the riverbank watching what they were doing. There were people on the shores. On this side were the ayahuasca people and on that side were the tobacco people, right? People on both sides, and I'm watching from over there. Then this short, fat guy comes out, all bitter, you know; it was the mother of ayahuasca. He grabs a rock, like this big, and throws it at the mother of tobacco. *Boom!* Tobacco, the man with the hat, he dodges; the rock goes *boom* and lands by his side. The other one grabs a metal bar, *boom* it goes; he throws the rod at him, but he also dodges it. There they are, bickering away, but neither gets up the courage to actually fight, since both are powerful. I'm right there, watching them. Then, I woke up and ahh... This is ayahuasca and tobacco fighting.

You can heal just using tobacco, tobacco is easy-peasy. If you don't have any ayahuasca left, you drink just a little bit and it'll teach you in your dreams. You chop it up, it has to be the one from the *mazo*,[87] if not, the tobacco that comes in a bag. You mash it up a bit mixed in water, you wring it out, and you take one sip. When there are sick people, one sip and with that, you heal, see. Tobacco teaches you. It gives you a power in your body; your spirit will have power, you see. With that alone you can already heal. You soak just one little serving and you wring it out, calculating one little shot glass. It's easy-peasy, but you do have to diet.

Then, with *agua florida*[88] too, one little glass, but that's strong, really strong. Also, pure alcohol with camphor;[89] you put it in the alcohol, drink one little cup and you can heal with that too. You don't need to have ayahuasca once you've learned how.

Do you know what tobacco is good for? You crush its fresh green leaves for the lazy ones, for the slackers, to cure them of that. You give them a good amount. It's like a purgative and they have to diet it strictly for eight days. Before that's over they already want to go out and do something; they break the diet and right away they're restless! That's raw tobacco, fresh, crushed and mixed with water; that's what you have to drink. And does it ever get rid of laziness! I want someone to give me some of that… Nobody knows this, only I understand about it. But—very careful with the diet, definitely.

Tobacco works for all kinds of things, see. For going into the forest: nothing will come after you. Don't leave your tobacco lying around just anywhere, because some idiot could be observing you and, *boom!* He'll grab you unawares if you don't have any tobacco. All those things you have to be careful about. But not me though,

---

87. Way in which black tobacco or *mapacho* is prepared, where the leaves of the plant are bound tightly in the shape of a short, thick log, which is cut with a knife to then be rolled into cigarettes.

88. Common perfume in Peru traditionally made with flower essence, often used for ceremonial or esoteric purposes.

89. The plant Ignacio refers to as camphor is *Faramea anisocalyx* (Rubiaceae), an Amazonian understory bush called *alcanfor*, whose aroma earned it the comparison to camphor (the unrelated *Cinnamomum camphora*), presumably by early Spanish arrivals.

I'm an ayahuasquero but I don't have tobacco on me in the forest. What favors me are my prayers; I go into the forest, I cross myself, and nothing bad happens to me. Snakes can be sleeping right there and they don't notice me either. Not a single insect gets stuck to your body. They fly away from you. Wherever you go, they're escaping from you. Tobacco is potent.[90]

And when you have a lot of sorrow, go to the path out there, smoking your cigarette. And the cigarette butt, with your left hand, *whoosh!*—you throw it over your shoulder. Repeat that three afternoons and forget it; you won't be remembering anyone. A really nice secret, that one. Learn it. That's what the apprentice-ship in the "occult sciences" is like… that's what this is called.[91]

---

90. Here Don Ignacio makes reference to a common local practice of carrying tobacco in the forest to repel snakes and other animals and spirits.

91. Ignacio would occasionally use the term "occult science" to refer to his form of shamanic knowledge and practices.

Tobacco, Tabaco, Mapacho (*Nicotiana tabacum*) →

Cashew, Marañón
Anacardium occidentale (Anacardiaceae)

There are some huge ones like this, and other smaller ones. It's a remedy against leishmaniasis.[92] Its resin burns much more than iodine.

---

92. Previously identified by its local name, uta, this flesh-eating disease transmitted by flies is found irregularly throughout the Amazon basin.

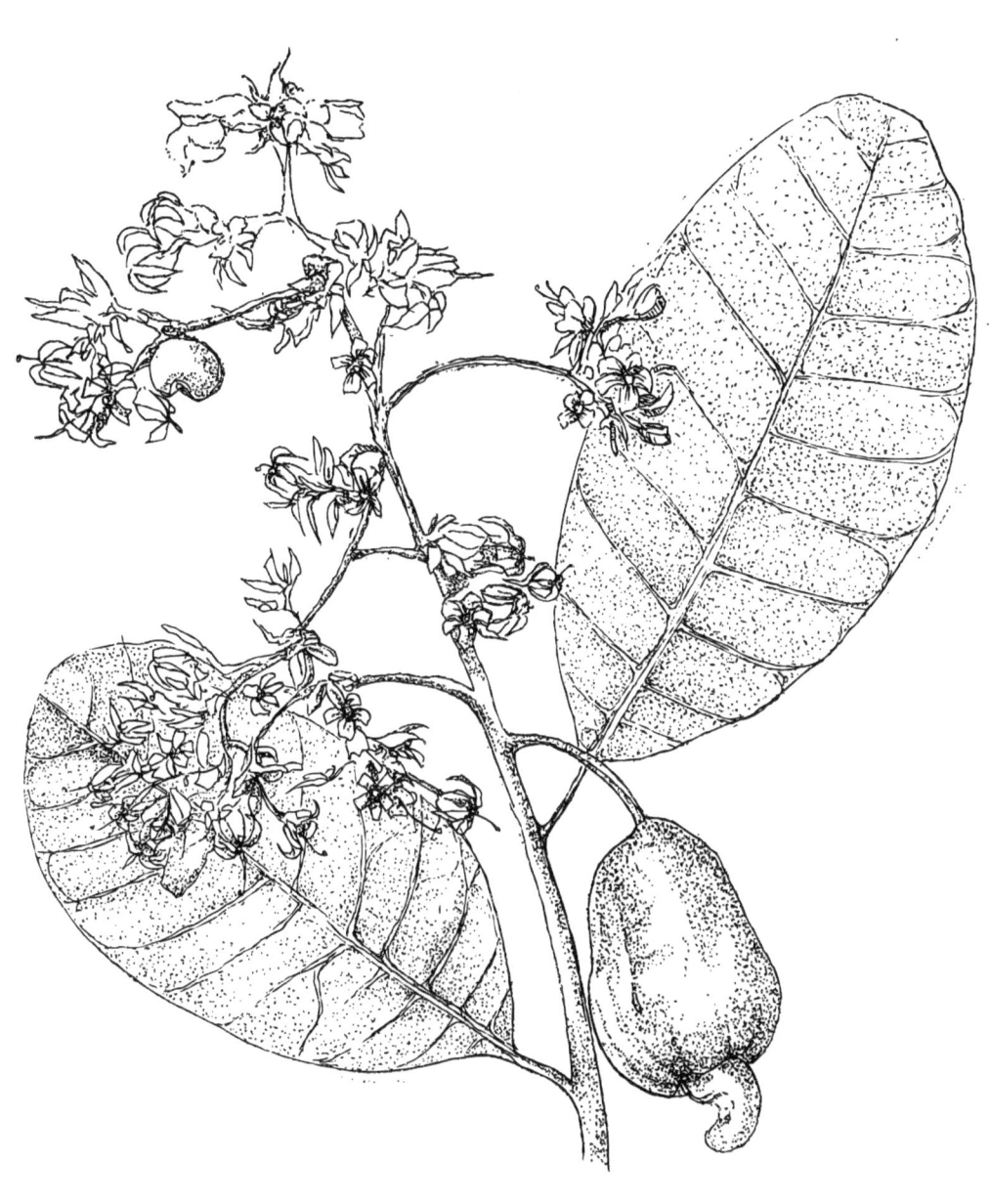

Chapumbilla, Sano Sano
Cyathea sp. (Cyatheaceae)

Chapumbilla is sano sano.[93] There is a male type and female, and they both work just as well. The female has thorns at the top. You just open it and chop it up. On the other hand, the male is long and has downy hairs on it. You cut that one, peel it, and its heart is soft. As a remedy, it's used to treat hemorrhage, for internal wounds, for cooling,[94] and to regulate the blood. Steeped it's a nice tea.

---

93. Sano sano is the common name for this plant in Madre de Dios, but Don Ignacio used to insist that its "correct" name was chapumbilla.
94. In traditional Peruvian herbal medicine, plants are recognized as being either hot or cold, or somewhere on a spectrum in between. "Hot" conditions can be counteracted with "cool" herbs and vice versa. Here sano sano is described as *fresco* (cool or cooling), whereas Don Ignacio would frequently remark that ayahuasca is *calida* (hot, heating), evidenced by the heat sensations and sweating induced in many who take it.

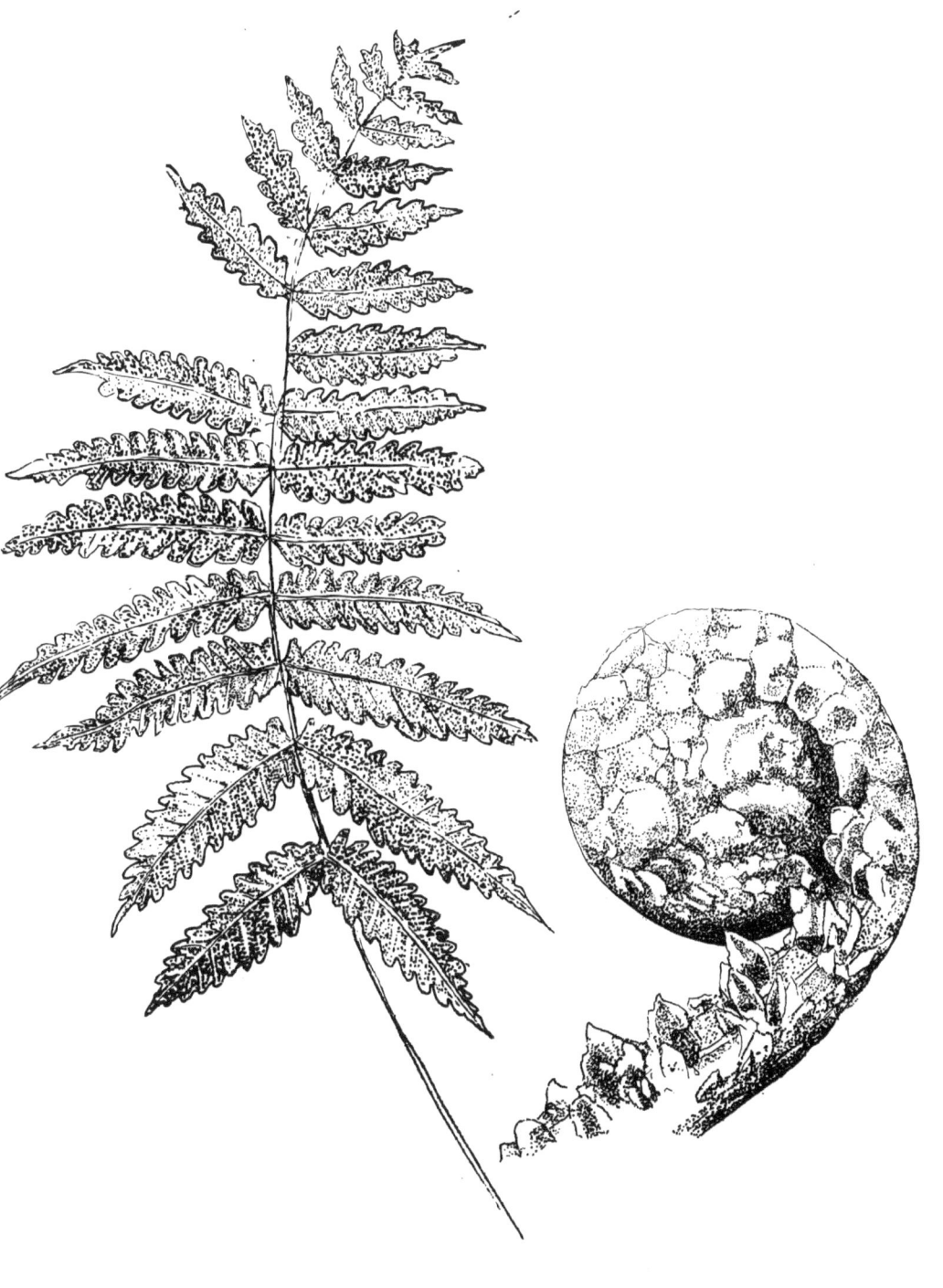

Clavo Huasca
Tynanthus panurensis (Bignoniaceae)

Clavo huasca is a thick liana; it's lovely that one, fragrant. They also say that extracting the juice itself from that one for ihuanasi[95] *is good, you can get an ihuanasi with that one.*

---

95. Woman, in the Ese'Eja language. Though Don Ignacio says here that clavo huasca is good for "getting women," the plant is also commonly used as a simple remedy (without diet) for erectile dysfunction.

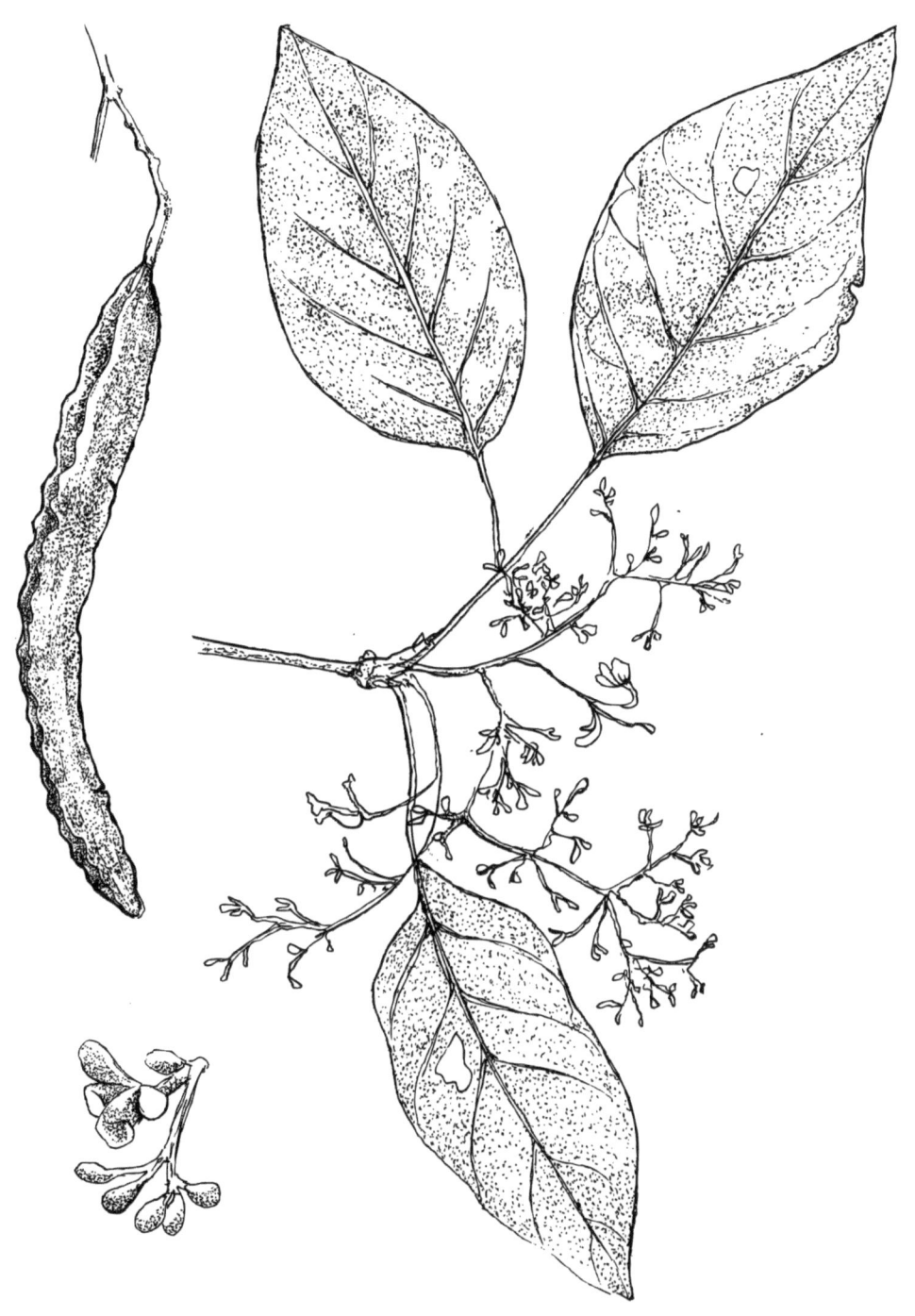

Coconilla
Solanum sessiliflorum (Solanaceae)

You bathe yourself with this to surround yourself with thorns, to defend yourself from the brujos. Nobody will get close to you when you drink ayahuasca.

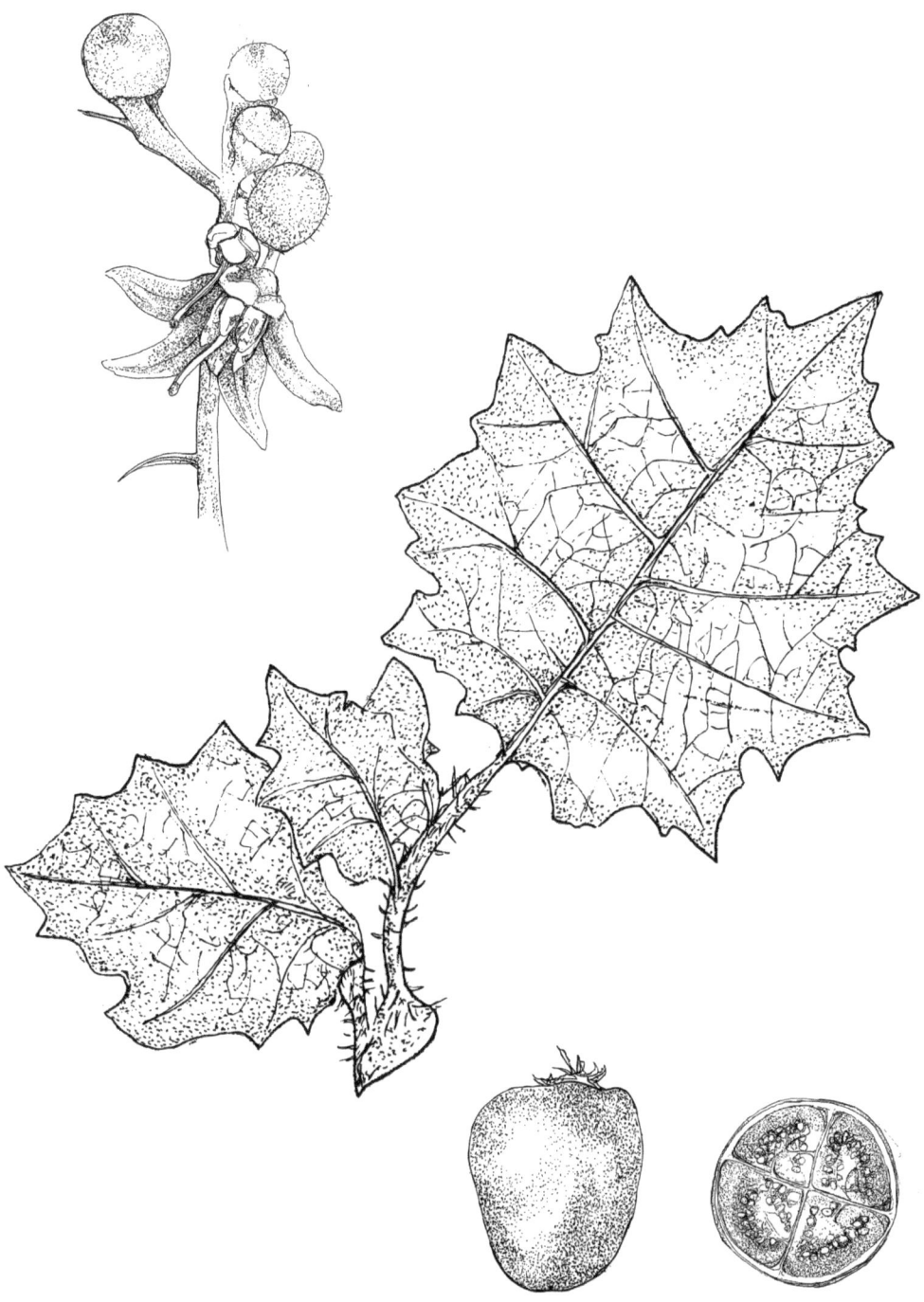

Cucaracha Huasca
Anemopaegma paraense (Bignoniaceae)

Cucaracha huasca has just a really nice smell, lovely. That one, if you want to alienate a person, you chew on it, dry that, and give it to them in powder-form. Just like you chew on your coca leaf powder, like that. That's what you give to the person that you want to hate you; you give it to him or her in a coffee or tea too, and: done. Get them to drink it, because it's chewed by you, right? That's what they're going to drink, and after four or five days, after a week she won't even want to see you. That's its recipe. I haven't tried it, but I've been guaranteed that it works.

And to cure dogs. If you cure a dog with that plant, nothing but deer is what it'll hunt for you. On the new moon, you put one teaspoon in its nose and another tablespoon in its mouth. Your dog has to be tied up for four days. Give him cold food, without any salt; they have their diet too. Grate it raw, and that, soaked in water, give it to your dog, but on the new moon. It'll catch the deer; it'll wear it down in a heartbeat! The deer runs like that; it comes back around to where it came from. It's not an animal that runs very far. When it's close to the river, if it jumps into the water even, even then the dog won't leave it; it'll follow it and if the deer swims off, it'll follow it along the edge of the water.

Cumala Colorada →
Iryanthera sp. (Myristicaceae)

Cumala colorada, for the facticos[96] the little ones have. Wet a bit of cotton with its resin and rub it on their mouth when little ones have facticos. But it's from this red variety, you put the red resin on there.

---

96. Ignacio uses an unfamiliar idiom to refer to canker sores and small, pimple-like infections of the gums.

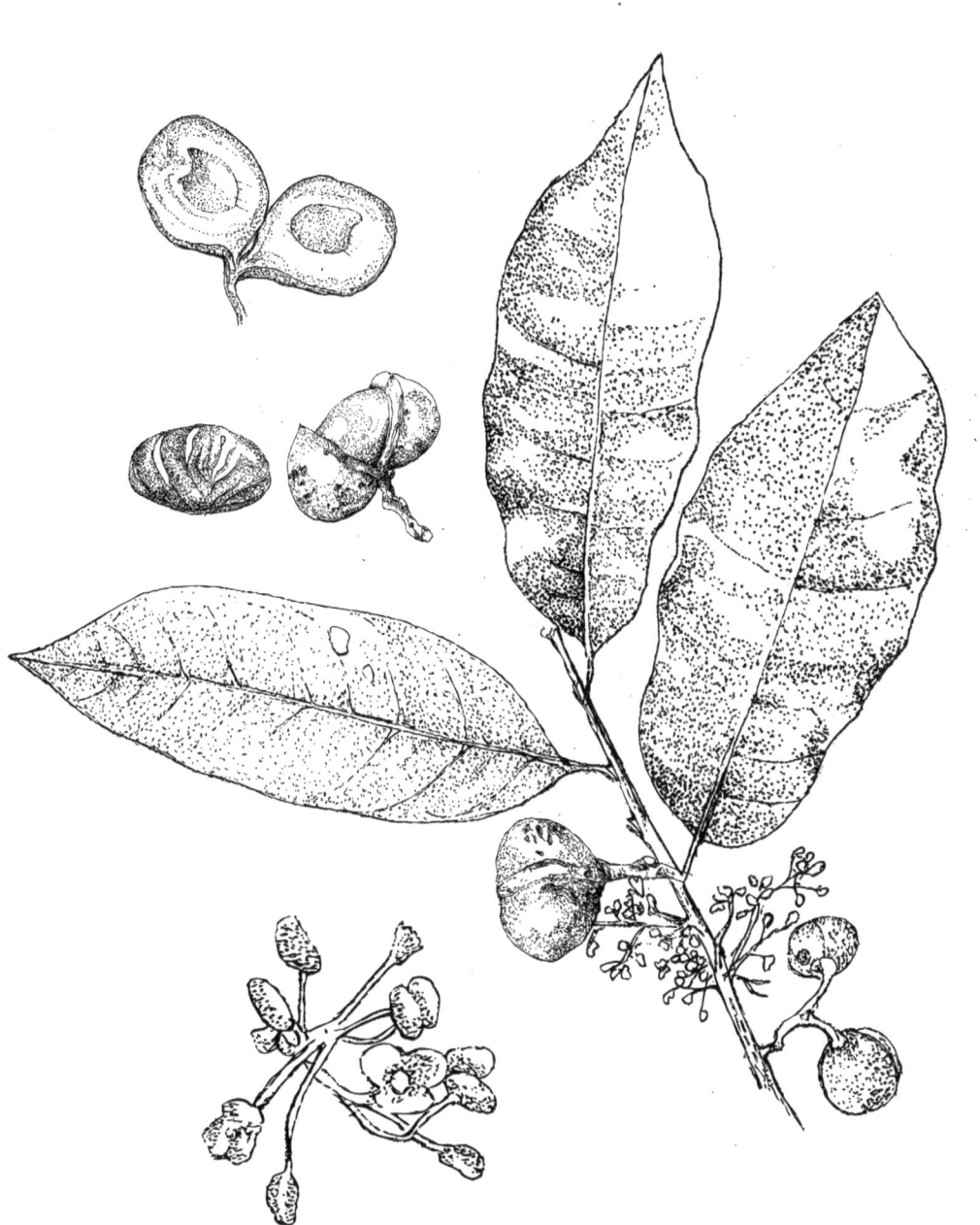

TEN

The Song of the Dead

After this life, there is no other life. Where could the spirit go? Nobody knows where the spirit goes. They say it goes to heaven. What heaven?! The spirit wanders around here, but where exactly? From time to time, it makes you dream and you meet with the spirits. How could there be a heaven?! They're such liars, those religious types.

One night I went to the cemetery. I had my radio. I went by myself with my radio at low volume,[97] sitting at the foot of the grave of the mother of my children. That's where I sat all night listening to the night. Around eleven o'clock I came back; I went to bed to go to sleep and that's when the wretched ones revealed themselves to me.

There was a guy called Oscar Valera. One year before he died; I saw him right there in my dream. And there they came, down a broad path, the dead were dancing with a yellow ribbon and singing very sadly. And I'm standing there by his side and I asked him, "Hey," I tell him, "what's all this?"

"There's going to be some little dead guy," he says to me, "but he's not going to work out. They're going to remove him and throw him into the river, into the water," he tells me.

And Walter's wife, that woman was going to give birth. Seven days after I did that work, she gave birth. A still birth. They threw the baby away, it died. That's what he was telling me, I guess.

---

97. Don Ignacio is making a double entendre here that he repeated on various occasions over the years. His "radio," which he also sometimes called his "record player" was his bundle of sanganga leaves (*Pariana* sp.) used in ceremonies as a rattle.

Then they started singing, and a woman approaches me.

"Are you okay?" she asks me.

"Yes, I'm fine."

And she asks me, "And do you know what this song is for?"

"No, no," I tell her.

"This song we're singing, you must learn it," she tells me. But it was a very sad song. "And you learn it and the girlfriend that has dumped you, go and you sing it to her; you dedicate that song to her, and she'll grab a knife and she will cut her own throat."

That's as far as I got, I never went to the cemetery again.

The dead teach you. I didn't want to continue, but the dead teach you. I don't want to go any higher in this science. I don't want to be evil, you see; it can teach you to be evil too. It must be that I'm tired now, see, I can hardly handle my science. You have to go through all kinds of shit to learn this crap. You have to take care of yourself. But, well, around here, people are very naughty, very harmful. They're envious.

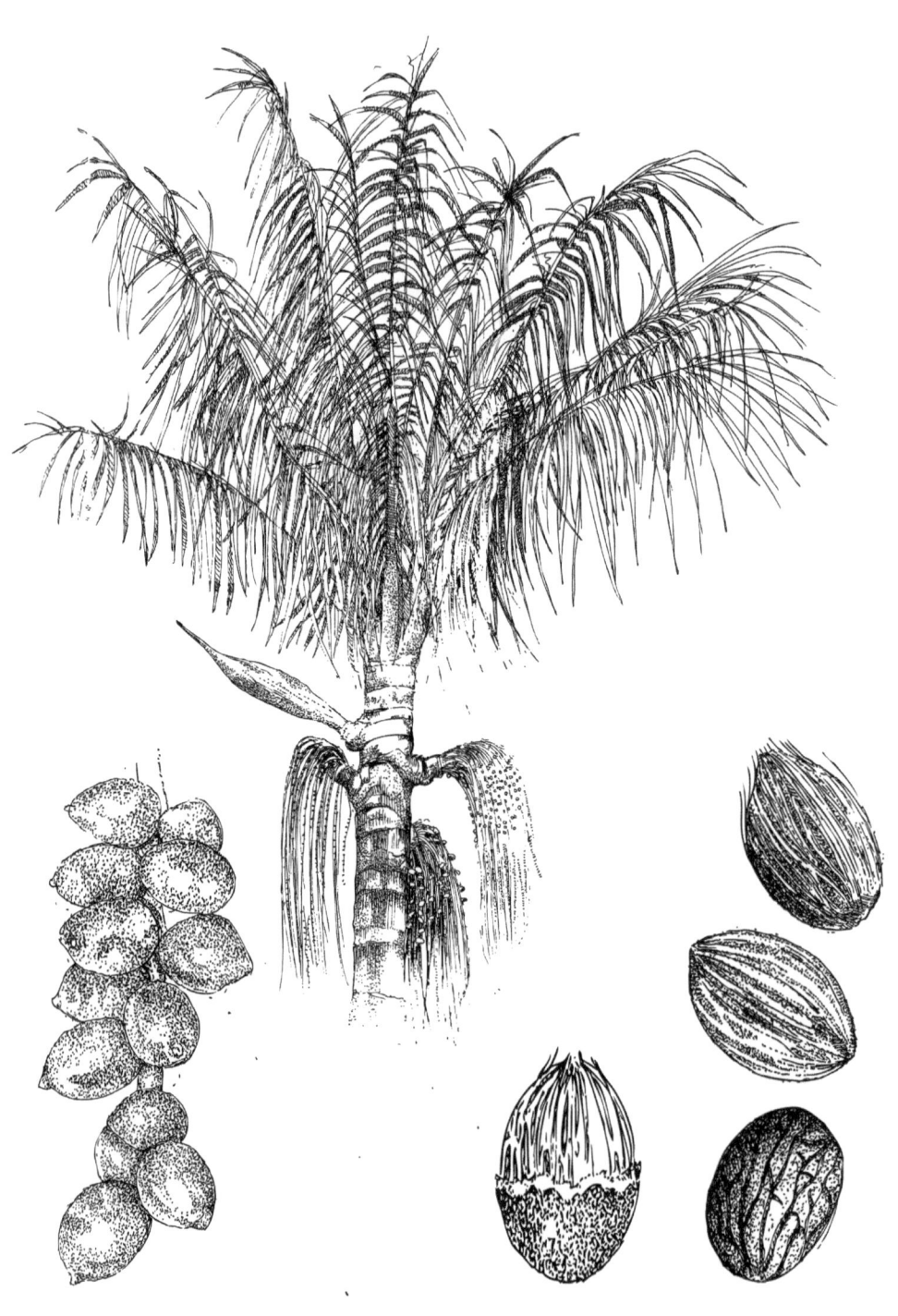

ELEVEN

The Mother of the Ungurahui Palm

I wonder what the mother of the abuta vine[98] is like? She must be good. She can be found, but nobody knows which one is her face. Well, not just anyone can know that. But looking for her, you'll get there! She shows you. You follow the plants. Looking at the plants you'll find her.[99]

Like the ungurahui palm's[100] mother; ungurahui's is a beautiful lady! But she has green hair. That plant almost killed me too, damnit. I was in bed for thirty days just for breaking off its underripe fruit.

There, close to the cemetery, right behind it, all of that used to be forest before, and that's where I knew of a trunk of ungurahui. At the time, my daughter who's in Lima, she was still little.

"Let's go, little one," I say to her, "let's go bring in ungurahui."

So we went.

I was healthy, man, just like I'm talking to you now. And that was the night I broke off a bunch of the fruit of the ungurahui. There were three bunches. The one I was going to cut was in the middle, and there was another green bunch over here. I had

---

98.   Medicinal liana, *Cissampelos pareira* (Menispermaceae).
99.   Essentially Don Ignacio is saying that, through visions in ceremonies and through dreams, one can eventually receive a vision of the mother of a plant.
100. Palm tree with delicious, oily fruits, *Oenocarpus bataua* (Arecaceae).

← Ungurahui (*Oenocarpus bataua*)

to hack that one away to get to the ripest bunch. Man, I hacked away and when I climbed down, I already had the shivers. Gosh, what's happening? I cut the bunch, it fell, and I climbed down.

"I've got the shivers," I tell my daughter. "I'm not well."

"What have you got, daddy?"

"I don't know, I think I got a fever," I tell her.

We gathered the ungurahui fruit. We came back. I got here with a bit of a fever. I went straight to bed, damnit.

The day after that, I think it was around this time of day when the motorboats were heading upriver. In those days, there wasn't a road yet.

I was in bed. They took me to Puerto Maldonado. I went to town and got to the Brazil nut camp owner's house.

"And what's up with you?" the old man says to me.

"I don't know what's wrong with me, Don Martín."

Martín was the old man's name.

"What have you got, then?"

"I've got the shivers."

"César!" he says to his son, "give him half a bottle of milk of magnesium in warm water."

So he prepared half a bottle for me. I drank it. My body felt nice at that moment; it was all calm again.

In those days, we used to come and go by river. I think we left at three and arrived here at the community at seven, after dark. Over there, where the boat landing is now, where Ernesto and Chiquilino's dad lived before. They lifted me up like dead weight from the canoe; they brought me here and: *boom!* Straight to bed, dang it.

For an entire month I was in bed. That's when I saw a beautiful woman in my dream.

"Why did you cut my hair?" was what she told me.

A beautiful woman, her hair was greenish, long hair, but good looking, you see! That's what she said to me. She made me ill.

The day after that, old Don Santiago came, the father of all these Durán kids. He was a good nurse technician. He was a policeman for the republic. Gosh, the old man was really a good guy. He cured me. He gave me some injections and that's how I got better. I had three illnesses apparently: the illness from that plant, the forest wanted to carry me off, and malaria too. Geeze, my tongue was so dry, my whole throat; I wanted to poison myself.

The late Campana, he also knew a little. That one, he only had to drink camphor to be able to heal others. But he prepared remedies. He'd ask for the plants, but he didn't know the forest. He didn't walk the forest capably. He ordered the plants and then prepared them. So this Campana came, he blew tobacco on me, and then he said, "You fool, the ungurahui almost carried you off."

Why did she turn bitter, though? Later, another fool also found the palm with bunches of fruit and also chopped them to the ground, and he didn't get sick; but I got sick.

At the time, my son Luchín was still little. I would always have a weapon on hand, since the huanganas[101] would cross the river there. One day I killed five of them! I was getting out of bed by then. I took all five of them to the boy.

"Go on, you skin them," I tell him. "I'm going to make jerky."

I just barely managed to make jerky out of the five huanganas.

They brought me food, but no way, I didn't eat, I was just moaning. One month I spent in bed. I escaped death by a hair's breadth. Since then, I haven't gotten sick again. I think when I get sick again, it'll be when I'll go. Jesus Christ will take me. I won't be taken by just anyone.

I had a thousand tobacco plants and man, when I got out of bed, they were totally bare! These massive worms! It was lost.

You have to inspect tobacco plants every day, because if a worm is there for two nights it'll totally strip a leaf. In two nights, the worms are already huge, too. But there's a secret for that: you gather the worms and you burn them on a Tuesday. Or with little girls—you get them to gather the worms and burn them right

---

101. White-lipped peccary. *Tayassu pecari.*

there and then, the little worms that they collect. Those worms are tiny right now, but the following day they'll be big. They fall to the ground and turn into butterflies.

When you're a newbie, you shouldn't offend the ungurahui. You have to get to know and understand it. In dreams and taking the plants you see them; even better, in dreams—but the ones after midnight. It advises you in a really lovely way in your dreams. What I can't learn is its songs, I'm such a dimwit. All the power that these plants have!

Tobacco, Tabaco, Mapacho (*Nicotiana tabacum*) →

TWELVE

A Floral Bath

Cordoncillo[102] is one of the best things to use for floral baths,[103] but you have to go for the ones that have a fragrance, not the ones that don't have any smell; they're no good— they have no strength. The aromatic ones are the ones that have strength and with these ones, well, they'll flock to you like bees go after… you know what I mean.

When I was at the mouth of the Malinowski,[104] I was there on my own for almost a year, see. There, a woman showed herself to me in a dream.

"Why do you suffer alone?" she says to me in my dream. "Do you know cordoncillo?"

"Yes, I know it."

"Get fourteen plants, but go for the ones that have a fragrance to them."

There are different types of cordoncillo plants. There are some that are vines, some are small trees. There are some with fuzzy leaves, others without hairs. There are large leaves and leaves of different colors. You bathe yourself with the plant in the new moon and, sheesh, they'll come after you like vultures! In the

---

102. Several species of the Piper genus, also known locally as matico or, at higher elevations, as moqo moqo.
103. *Baños de florecimiento* or floral baths are traditional ritual applications of plants extracted in water, hot or cold depending on the plant, to confer medicinal and spiritual benefits.
104. Where the Malinowksi River flows into the Tambopata, department of Madre de Dios.

← Various species of cordoncillo or matico (*Piper* sp.)

late afternoon, at around six in the evening, you scrub the leaves thoroughly in water. That water will become very fragrant. Wash yourself with it, but don't remove the pieces of leaves left clinging to you. Stand there for a while dressed only in that, then put your clothes on and immediately go to bed. Diet for four days, concentrated, tucked away without anyone seeing you. And you have to eat food without any salt, without fat, without any seasoning. Shoot, you'll be fine after that.

Even to this day, they're still arriving at my house, and it's been over ten years! This little herb is still working. But I say, for what? I'm old now; it's over now. If I were your age, what wouldn't I do with these plants…

It's therapeutic and it's attractive to women. It's a remedy for love as well as for pain in your bones, and colds—a steam bath with this one. The pigeons will flock to you just like how you see them in the main square in Cusco.

I tried it in Malinowski. Then, when I came back, I said, "Heck, why did I bathe myself with these plants?" As I said, this plant is the best, nothing like those other herbs. I do prepare the other herbs, yes, to sell. But what happened if I were to use all these plants myself? *Boo!* No, I don't like that.

Ayahuasca teaches you all sort of things, see.

THIRTEEN

Mrs. Abuta

Abuta[105]—this lady, this plant—is very powerful. As a remedy you have to take it for up to a month, or for only fifteen days. It's good for internal wounds; for those that are coughing up blood from the lungs; for chronic bleeding in women; also for lesions on the skin. For fever, you take it by the drop. For the little kiddos it's good too. That's its power.

I was taught this one by Rafael Paya. I went to saw wood way up the Madre de Dios River and he says he healed himself with abuta from when he was coughing up blood. There was this other guy... I don't know what that guy's name was, but he tells him, "Take this, you idiot! I know this herb, and it's a really good one," he tells him.

He prepared a bottle for him, and he got better just by drinking that! It's really good. I don't know where that guy might be now.

I healed Doña Isabel with this plant. That lady liked to go out walking in the *aguajal*.[106] It seems that one day she went to the aguajal that we have in the community, and gosh, there was a boa[107] there. It looks at her; the boa is watching her. I guess it was waiting for her, and then it got out of there, it left. Then in her dreams, she saw how the boa went right past her and she pressed up tight against a tree when the boa moved past her.

---

105. Woody liana, *Cissampelos pareira* (Menispermaceae).
106. An *aguajal* is a forest type found in swamps or seasonal wetlands dominated by the aguaje palm, *Mauritia flexuosa* (Arecaceae).
107. Anaconda or *boa de agua*. *Eunectes murinus* (Boidae).

She came to see me. I blew smoke on her only once, and she got a bit better. Then later she got sick again, she had a fever that wouldn't go down and a headache. Then she called for me to come and I went to see her. Gosh, the lady was moaning and groaning.

"Let's see, ma'am, I'm going to bathe you with some plants, maybe that'll do you good," I told her. I left.

I found a plant, as big as this, thick, fat. I brought a few big pieces of it. I got here and I pounded it. You prepare it for baths in just the same way you would prepare it for a remedy; you just mash it well, boil it, let it cool down a little and you bathe yourself with it, as hot as your body can handle. *Oof*, this is a real kicker of a remedy, this abuta. I called for her daughter, María, and she came.

"You're going to bathe your mother, as hot as her body can handle," I told her.

She took the water from here while it was still hot.

"And after the bath, you'll give her a little cup to drink."

I gave it to her in a little bottle. She took it over to her and gave her a bath with it.

The following day, since I had brought lots, I boiled more. I had her rest one day, and then the next day I gave her the other bath. That's when I went to see her. The fever and the headache had already gone away. What she felt was hunger, the lady says, geeze. That's when I told her.

"Let's go to my house, ma'am," I said to her, "You'll be with me there. What I eat, what those who take ayahuasca eat, that's what I'll give you. Maybe one of the visitors[108] will feel sorry for you and give you a couple of dollars," I tell her.

The lady didn't say anything in response.

She still needed one more bath, so I went out into the forest early the next day. I didn't have any more of the plant so I went to

---

108. Like others in the region, Ignacio referred to foreign visitors coming to his home for ceremony as *pasajeros*, literally passengers, meaning tourists.

get some. I pounded it, prepared it, put out the fire and went over to tell María. I got to the house and there was nobody there.

There was a guy there next to her house, at the boat landing.

"And where are these people?" I tell him.

"They've just left, Don Ignacio. They went to go logging."

"And the sick lady?"

"They took her too," he says.

Now the old lady is screwed!

"The sick lady is screwed now," I tell him.

"Why?" he asks.

"Of course, she was under treatment," I tell him. "She's screwed now."

It took them seven days; after seven days they came back and the old lady just couldn't... She got her daughter to call for me and I went to see her. She didn't get up, didn't answer when they called her. She was lying on her cot, face-down, moaning. Her daughter tells me, "And how do you think she's doing, Don Ignacio?"

"Why did you take her up there, then? Your mom no longer has any life left in her; she'll be gone in five days," I tell her. "Why did you take her, didn't you see that she was in the middle of a treatment? You should have talked to me before taking her!" I tell her. "I had actually told her to come to my house, because she told me that sometimes you don't have anything to eat," I said to her daughter.

She didn't say anything.

That's where it all ended. She died four days after I went to see her. They made the lady suffer, goddamnit, so, so much. The lady had a relapse, and the relapse is hard. She only needed one more bath, after that it was just food. That's why I told her, come to my house; there's always enough food here. I have rice. When I bring home rice, I bring a whole sack.

When you're in treatment, well, that's just the worst! Don't play around with plant remedies. If you're going to take it, you must diet it. And if you don't diet, it won't do you any good. On the contrary, it'll harm you. These people over here are depraved, geeze. If you tell them: you have to do it, don't do that... Man, I don't know, they sleep without any underwear on! ...

That's what these people are like. You know, I've seen it all! That's why I can say these things. They're terrible sinners from the time they're children, damnit.

Abuta (*Cissampelos pareira*) →

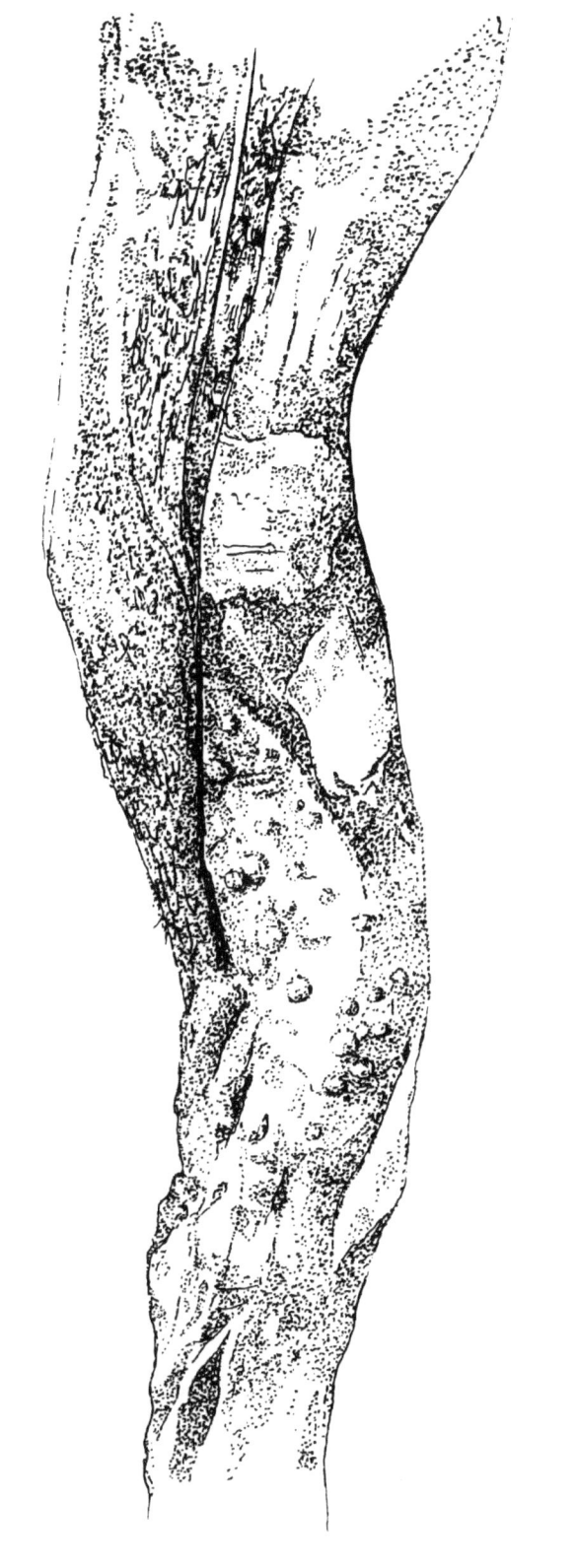

Chiric Sanango
Brunfelsia grandiflora (Solanaceae)

This is prepared to be taken in fingernail-sized amounts; you take just a small amount of the liquid, but the diet is thirty days. It gets rid of all the pains you have and also teaches you what you're going to do. That's its power. Its root, you grate it in water, you dissolve it in there and measure out the amount you're going to drink.

There's another one that's called sanango, I think. That one's for learning too. That one's a purgative. That one, shoot, you have to drink it and diet it; that's when it will teach you.

Estoraque
Myroxylon balsamum (Fabaceae)

Estoraque has a resin that's very fragrant. That's where the collared peccary washes itself; the coati[109] rubs itself with it too, where it's fragrant.

To treat leishmaniasis, apply it with cotton at the end of a little stick. It's like bushmaster[110] oil too. You have to wash the wound well, and only apply it on the wound itself. Its wood too, it's really good for sugar cane press rollers, the best wood for that.

---

109. *Nasua nasua*, a rainforest mammal known in Peru as achuñi or achuni.
110. Venomous rattlesnake, *Lachesis muta*; in Peru, shushupe. One of the most aggressive, dangerous vipers of the Amazon, the lard or oil extracted from its body is used for several medicinal applications.

Huasaí →
Euterpe precatoria (Arecaceae)

Hierba de Loro
Peperomia sp. (Piperaceae)

When you have enemies, you bathe yourself, rubbing yourself with the leaves, and you go to see your enemy. They'll end up liking you. Bathe yourself with that plant, go to visit them, and they'll say, "Come in, have a seat." To attract friendship, to forget about arguments—it makes the enemy forget. Do you know what its process is? Look, say I'm the boyfriend of a girl, and her mother, her family don't like me. I bathe myself with that one, I get there, and I sort of act the fool, strolling around them three times, around the mother, the father, the whole family and: done! There is some around here too, but you have to look for it; it's difficult to find. It's a little vine.

A driver for a hotel, this guy was almost left by his wife because he was dieting; he was already sad, see! One day he came here with his pistol, damnit, wanting to kill himself, to commit suicide, saying that if he found his wife with another man, he would kill them both.

"Don't be an idiot," I told him, damnit. "How many times have they done that to me. Just you wait and see, damnit," I tell him.

I went into the forest, I brought him the herb.

"I'll bring you some herbs, bathe yourself with them and when you get home, if your missus is there, discreetly walk around her three times, counter-clockwise," I told him. "Don't pay her too much attention when she talks to you. You can answer but act aloof. Walk around her like you're looking at the floor searching for something, that's how you circle around her three times."

He got home to where his wife was. She talked to him; he hardly answered. He already had that secret with him. Then, at night, he bathed himself again, and the following day he was already making tsojó.[111] And, well, he got married! That's where he is today, with his little missus, he ended up marrying. The guy thanked me for it.

---

111. Sex in the Ese'Eja language.

Ishpingo
Amburana cearensis (Fabaceae)

Ishpingo is perfume-like, its bark and everything. When you boil the bark of that one, the liquid turns black when you boil it; you purify that and let it thicken. For tobacco, when you make tobacco, when you press it up to cure the leaves,[112] you add that plant, you sprinkle it on like honey and knead it in well, you see. Geeze, you cut it up and you're smoking over here and they can smell you way over there. The people all the way over there can smell it, nice and fragrant. It also has its seed; you make those into powder, and you can make that into a perfume in alcohol. You rub it on yourself and it's very fragrant. It's nice for wood too, its wood is shiny. After planing, it has a very shiny finish.

---

112. Don Ignacio would prepare *mazo de tabaco*, literally a "mallet" or "club" of tobacco, made by pressing together tobacco leaves to form a dense, tightly bound log, left for several months to cure and improve in flavor. He would sometimes add wild honey, sugar cane alcohol, or ishpingo extract to the leaves when building the mazo.

Jergón Sacha
Dracontium sp. (Araceae)

Jergón sacha is for aches and pains. It's good to macerate it in alcohol. The other day I went to Gatica's; there was a man there and his feet looked like snake scales. He was treating him and he asks me:

"What could be good?" he says to me.

"Let's see, try jergón sacha."

And he was cured by washing himself with that. It's an antidote for poisonous snakes too, that one. You use the tuber; it has a tuber too, that one.

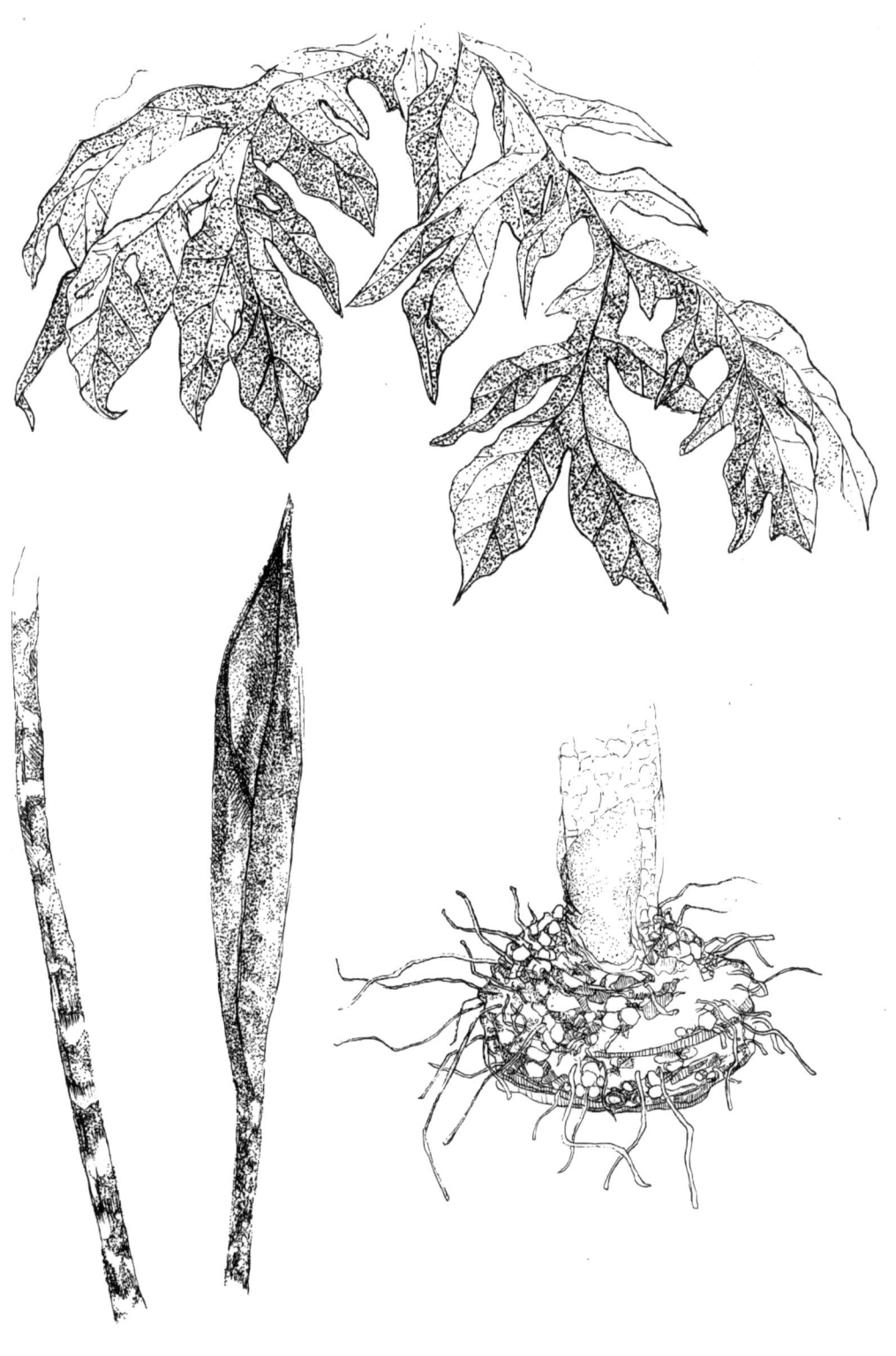

FOURTEEN

Prayer

Rihui can't be healed by hitting it with ishanga;[113] rihui is healed by praying, and there are also plants to put on it. Rihui sacha:[114] that one heals the rihui outbreak. It has its little fruit, like a kind of little red tomato. But I've healed more by using prayer. The majority of illnesses, I heal with prayer.

Rihui has the characteristic that once it breaks out and once it has made a circle around your body, you're on your way to Kaway[115] for him to do your hair. Rihui is very painful, like fire!

Evaristo had rihui; he was very sick from it. From here, he went off to see Flores and Flores examined him.

"Man, they've put a curse on you! Duri is putting a curse on you," he tells him. He didn't put anything on the rihui.

Then he went to Panduro and talked to him.

"Have you been seen by anyone?"

"Yes, I had Flores examine me."

"And what did he say to you?"

"He thinks I've been cursed—Duri is cursing me," he says.

---

113. *Rihui*, also known as *culebrilla*, is the local name for an infectious disease caused by the virus *Herpes zoster*. Ishanga (*Urera caracasana* - Urticaceae) is a variety of Amazonian nettle, the irritating leaves of which are used (in this case, erroneously) to hit and/or rub the area affected by the outbreak of rihui (an action called "*ishanguear*," which is in fact an effective treatment for some other conditions).

114. Herbaceous vine, *Solanum barbeyanum* (Solanaceae).

115. When Don Ignacio was asked about the identity of this Kaway, he explained that he was the Japanese immigrant running the first funeral home in Puerto Maldonado. This Kaway, it would seem, only gave haircuts to the dead.

← Rihui Sacha (*Solanum barbeyanum*)

Panduro examined him.

"What do you mean this is a curse? This is rihui!"

He prescribed him some herbs, and he got a little better. Then he comes here and tells me.

"They say you've cursed me. Heal me," he says.

"And what did Panduro say?"

"That I've got rihui."

"And that's what you've got, man! Why do you get caught up in those tales they tell you? I could heal you right here, but you've gone way over there," I tell him.

I did two afternoons of prayer and he healed completely with that.

Catahua (*Hura crepitans*) →

FIFTEEN

The Gringo and the Catahua

This tree is activated poison: its resin, the milk of the cata-hua.[116] One little teaspoon is its dose. It makes you purge from both ends. Before breakfast, of course—all purgatives must be taken before breaking your fast. You're going to diet it for about eight days after the purge: *warmi*, fats. Fats are cheese, butter, milk, all those things, but the toughest thing for a diet is *warmi*... woman![117]

It's a good purgative, but you have to follow what the person giving it to you tells you. Don't go close to the fire under any circumstance. Just respond to nature's call and go back to bed. Not just anyone can serve you this purgative.

There's an advertisement right now in Puerto Maldonado from someone who claims that they attract girls, call in women, with catahua. What idiots! How's that going to attract anyone? This is poison, you see! It's all advertising, that is. This has the property of poisoning the blood, killing the parasites that we have in the blood. In the blood we have these kinds of small bugs, really tiny like chiggers,[118] you see, really small, right? They live there in the blood and this one poisons them. These parasites are drinking

---

116. Tree. *Hura crepitans*. (Euphorbiaceae).
117. *Warmi* is Quechua for "woman" or "wife." Don Ignacio would often use the word as shorthand for the need to abstain from sex while dieting.
118. Isango in the local Spanish. Type of mite. *Trombicula autumnalis*.

your blood; they drain all your energy. They leave you without any courage.

When we're healthy our body is lit up by lights that are pure, and when we're sick you can barely see the light in our body because we're sick.

In Bolivia, there was this *gringo*, right?—I guess he was American, I don't know—and they say that gringo had this disease. Over there in Brazil, in Bolivia, I think there's this disease that eats away at your fingers: leprosy. And when a human has those kinds of wounds, it smells terrible.

The people around were disgusted by the gringo. They loathed him, they berated him, they kicked him out of the house. His finger was already totally eaten away.[119] The gringo was living there on his own, just sitting around.

He asked a rubber tapper for an axe, a machete, a pot and a bunch of thin plantains. He took his bed and went to a Brazil nut camp.

In Bolivia, there's lots of catahua in all the *bajío*;[120] Bolivia is low, see. And there was the gringo. He didn't have a gun, so he fished by bleeding catahua; with that he poisoned the stream, and he ate from that.[121] After a month in the forest, he looked at his wounds on his foot and his hand and they were drying out. They say that after three months he came out, completely cured. The gringo only ate fish with thin plantain; he was on a diet without even knowing it. The gringo got better. He went back to his country. Who knows? Maybe he's still there now, alive.

There are three varieties of catahua: black, yellow and white. The black and the white ones are thorny. The yellow is the best one, see; that one doesn't have much meat,[122] good for making canoes.

---

119. He uses the word *chuto*, or missing a part, like a dog without a tail.
120. Low terrace or flood plain forest, where catahua is found.
121. The resin of catahua is used as a fish poison, similar to barbasco, stunning the fish who ingest it and rendering them easy to capture.
122. By *carne* (meat), Don Ignacio probably means the bark and sapwood (alburnum), discarded in favor of the heartwood (duramen), more durable in water for boatbuilding.

To use catahua for fishing you have to bleed it. You have to extract a lot if it's for a large lake. Once in Mavila I fished at this lady's place. She was a widow. She took me there to make canoes at her house. I went there and stayed at her house for three months.

"Don Ignacio, so-and-so is going to come to harvest catahua," she says to me.

I don't know what his name was. He was a native.

"Let's go fishing at the lake. Go help him get the catahua," she says.

"Alright then."

The lady had good axes and she gave me tins that held a kilo each. You carve some little channels into the trunk, you put the axe to it starting from the bottom and making a little ladder all the way up. The milk will run down from there. Leave it there funneling in, and when you go to pick up the can, it'll be full. The following day, we carried off fourteen tins—a ton, since it was for a lake! I think it was on the second or third day after we released it that three canoes entered the lake. You mix it with the mud itself and sprinkle the catahua in the water. That day, only small fish died.

The following day her son-in-law says to me, "Don Ignacio, let's go and see how the lake is doing."

Dang, all of the fish were there floating belly up, all dead! Off to load them all into a canoe. There was a whole canoe-full of fish to take out to the riverbank! Then back we go, to pick up some more. There were tons on the surface of the lake and so we piled them all up. And that lady was very skilled at curing fish. Geeze, by the time we were bringing the next load of fish back, she had already made a ton of cured fish. Heck, I ate lots of fish that time. Good times, damnit.

Catahua (*Hura crepitans*) →

SIXTEEN

Bellaco Caspi

Bellaco caspi[123] is a tree, too. It's also a very strong purgative for pains and for the joints. You grate a certain amount of the bark and prepare it as a remedy. *Oof*, its effects start after about twenty minutes. It wipes you out. Its diet is for a month. With rheumatism and arthritis, when it's all knobby looking, it'll disappear by itself. Its resin is for fractures, sprains, for back pain; the resin is good for all kinds of things. For tumors you also stick the resin on it, to make *chupos*[124] mature, as we call them. You leave a circle in the middle for it to breathe and surround it with the milk, absorbing the swelling.

My mother had arthritis. She had the habit—since she had fourteen children—to give birth and three days later she'd be there washing with rainwater. That's what caused her the knobby appearance of her hands, her fingers, her feet, her knee. She was all hunched up. Rainwater is poisonous to humans. She collected the rainwater to wash. She could hardly walk. When we came to Peru, she was walking very slowly. She wasn't well.

And we arrived here, and that tree exists over there in Bolivia and over here too, it's everywhere, so I already knew about it. We gave her the purgative, only two tablespoons of its bark, grated and

---

123. Tree. *Himanthus sucuuba* (Apocynaceae).
124. Abscess or boil caused by infections in the blood, sometimes referred to by Ignacio as tumors.

← Bellaco Caspi (*Himanthus sucuuba*)

mixed in water. There's not much of a diet for that one when it's raw. The diet is stricter if you take it cooked. She got better. After three months she was back to going to the farm patch to weed.

Sangre de Grado (*Croton lechleri*) ➔

SEVENTEEN

Sangre de Grado

I used to fell sangre de grado[125] trees to get a liter; a large tree yields one liter. When the bottle is large, this tree will fill it up. You have to cut into it with a blade, then you put a little cup there and you slash it all up, and you collect it in a bottle. They grow in these bajíos. Gosh, and once it flowers, how fast their babies grow!

There's one that has very thin bark which doesn't have a lot of "milk." The one with double thick bark is the best; that one gives a lot of milk.

You take it by the drop for cancer. You have to mix it with cat's claw.[126] It's good for the lungs, for pain in the bones, for cuts too. It heals a cut in a heartbeat. I once prepared it for the mother of my children in wine, in a bottle. I served her; I think it was three little cups of sangre de grado and I gave it to her. Darn, she said it made her dizzy... One day she tells me, "I don't want to take any more. That remedy is no good; it wipes me out," she tells me.

And one morning, I go for it. I say, "I'm going to try this remedy."

Geeze, after a while I was falling apart. It's a lot—it's strong! It gives you terrible side effects, damnit. It knocks you out. It was like I had lost all of my bones. That's why I say you should only take it by the drop.

---

125. Tree. *Croton lechleri* (Euphorbiaceae).
126. Uña de gato. Woody liana. *Uncaria tomentosa* and *U. guianensis* (Rubiaceae).

When you harvest it, it can last a long time. Sheesh… and it even dries out! And then you have to add boiled water. Stored in a little bottle, it will keep its strength for years, but you have to preserve it. It's better if you add alcohol. Then it won't lose its strength.

That sangre de grado that they sell over there in Maldonado? It isn't pure. I'm already on to them. Starting with the leaves, they cook the whole leaf. They even use the little fruit pod it has. They make it from that. It's not pure, water with a bit of color is all it is. No… remedies shouldn't be mixed.

Manchinga
Brosimum alicastrum (Moraceae)

Manchinga is a large tree. Its resin is good for making into a poultice. It's one that has milk. The ashes contain nutrients for the plants. You just have to throw the ashes around the plants. That plant maintains them; it fertilizes the soil.

When this tree bears fruit, it gives a little white nut. My mother told me that in the time of the war between Paraguay and Bolivia— she was little, and there wasn't anything to eat, you see—they would collect the fruit from the manchinga, toast it, and they would eat it.

It's edible, that seed. It's tasty. It's a little spongy. That jungle in Bolivia is low; throughout that whole jungle there is manchinga, enormous trees all over the place. The peccaries eat them, all sorts of animals do. The resin works well stuck on your skin too.

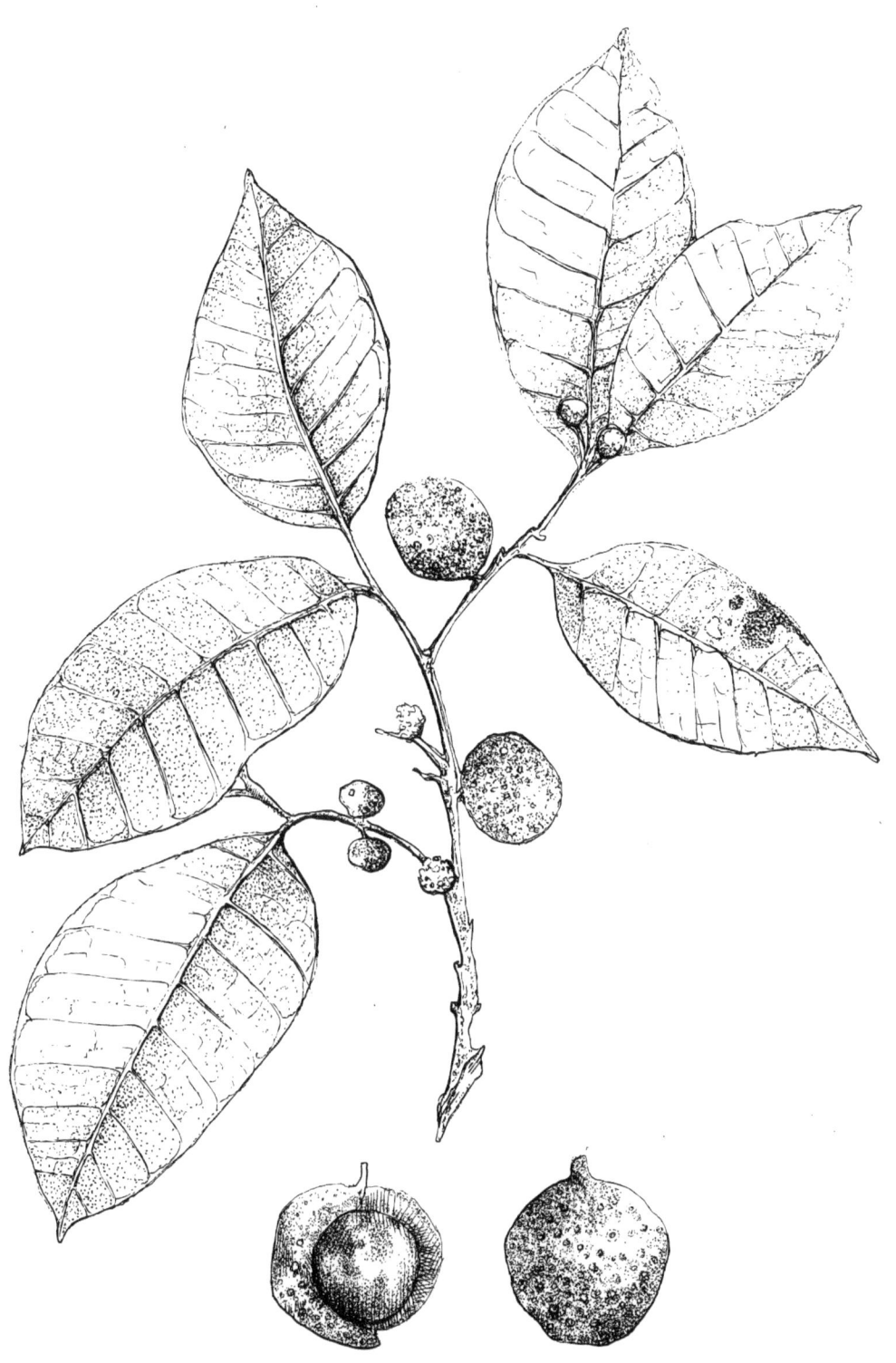

Mashonaste
Clarisia racemosa (Moraceae)

Mashonaste is a tree to make into a poultice. You apply its resin, but don't take it off until it falls off by itself, because that's what absorbs; it absorbs your pains. It's as if it pulls them from you. It makes tumors[127] shrink or makes them mature very small. I say, preparing the bark of its root to drink can be good too.

A lady brought two doctors from Lima and I shared this one with them. They've sent me many greetings and gratitude because it took their back pain away.[128]

This is an excellent tree for injuries, for all types of sprains and fractures. It's good for everything, this one, because it adjusts you. It pulls on you. Nice tree, eh!

---

127. Abscesses or boils caused by infections in the blood, sometimes called tumors by Ignacio.
128. One of the authors witnessed just such a visit to Don Ignacio from doctors from Lima. They referred to him respectfully as an "expert traumatologist, for his treatment of injuries that would have taken at least twice as long to heal using familiar conventional medicine." The patient in question had received poultices of mashonaste and renaquilla resin on a multiple-fractured and dislocated shoulder.

Ninacaspi[129]
Capparis sp. (Capparaceae)

This plant is good for treating fungal infections when they're on your feet. You grate its root, make it into a poultice by adding a little bit of water, and you wrap it around your foot where the fungal infection is, nice and hot, but only until it heats up. If it heats up too much, you have to remove it or it'll make your skin blister.

This plant's root is straight, deep; you pull it up, but you can't break it off just like that! That's very hard to do! You remove the dirt and then you grate it very finely and leave it in hot water to soak. Put in as much in as you want. It doesn't have to boil.

I had an uncle in Bolivia and he plays a trick on this guy; he tells him, "This is good for making your penis get bigger. Tie it on," he tells him, "but this one burns!"

And, well, the dummy tied it on.

"You're going to take it off when it starts to burn too strong."

"Alright then," he says.

And geeze, he tied it on and the following day he couldn't even walk, damnit. He had gotten blisters all over. This one burns, see! And so the guy couldn't walk to go and clear his farm.[130] It was August and "Casa Suárez" used to have an enormous farm back then. And the lady in charge, I don't know what her name was, asks, "And why is he not coming?"

"He's ill."

"What's wrong with him? He should get seen by the nurse practitioner."

So he goes. He's having trouble walking; he had a massive blister right in the middle! Right there and then, the nurse pricked him. Drained it and gave him some medicine so he would heal.

---

129. In Amazonian Quechua, ninacaspi means "fire tree" due to the heat and even chemical burns that can be caused by the root's powerful phytochemistry.
130. Here, in keeping with the story's location in Bolivia, Ignacio uses the Bolivian word, *chaco*, for farm.

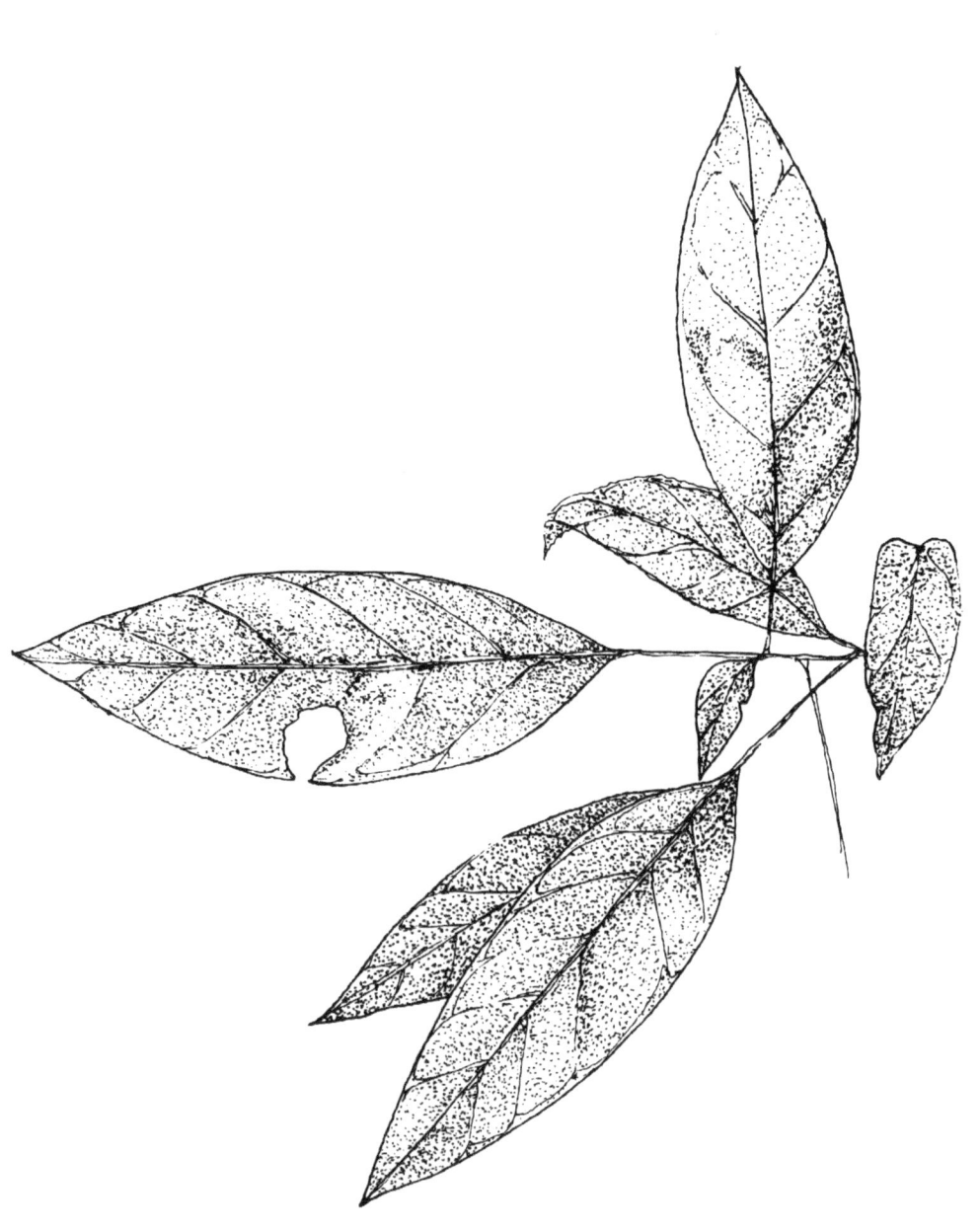

Ojé
Ficus insipida (Moraceae)

You extract the resin from ojé and you store it for four days. On the fifth day, at four in the morning, the person who's going to give it to you will come at that time to serve it to you.

Its diet is strict, for eight days. On the eighth day, you bathe yourself with the boiled leaf of the same tree so that it doesn't mess you up too much. On the diet you eat little salt, little sugar, but also you avoid other things like pork fat. Even worse if you have tsojó; it'll make you fat in a heartbeat, like filled with air. And if the person that serves it to you doesn't know how to cure you, you'll be on your way to Kaway for a hair cut.

For a complete treatment as a purgative, just four teaspoons, but that one leaves you... oof! It burns your anus, damn it. It burns like hell! They served it to me when I was a boy.

To have children, you take ojé without dieting; that heats up the ovaries. By the teaspoonful in the early mornings, you start with one teaspoon, then two, three, four, up to six. Then, from six you go back to five, four, three, two, down to one. There's no diet, except for making love, because if you do that it'll make you fat right away, full of air, and if the one who served you doesn't know what he's doing, it'll kill you.[131] You have to go to see the person that gave you the remedy to cure you and then you'll drink boiled ojé with a very strict diet for it to heal you.

That one too, if you want to learn from it, you have to look for one that's of a decent size, a good one, right? Not just any ojé, because there's one that's got smaller leaves; the milk of that one is yellow. That one's very strong, you see; it burns way too much! For you to learn from ojé you have to go to the tree to extract a teaspoon of it every morning. After a year it'll already be withering. See by then you're already killing it.

---

131. Clearly, to use ojé as a remedy for infertility in women does not imply trying to conceive during or immediately after the course of treatment, which requires strict abstention from sex as a key part of this kind of treatment.

When its leaves have fallen, that's when you stop drinking it. This one's a good doctor. You diet the whole year until you kill it, but you don't get sick, you see. It's healing you.

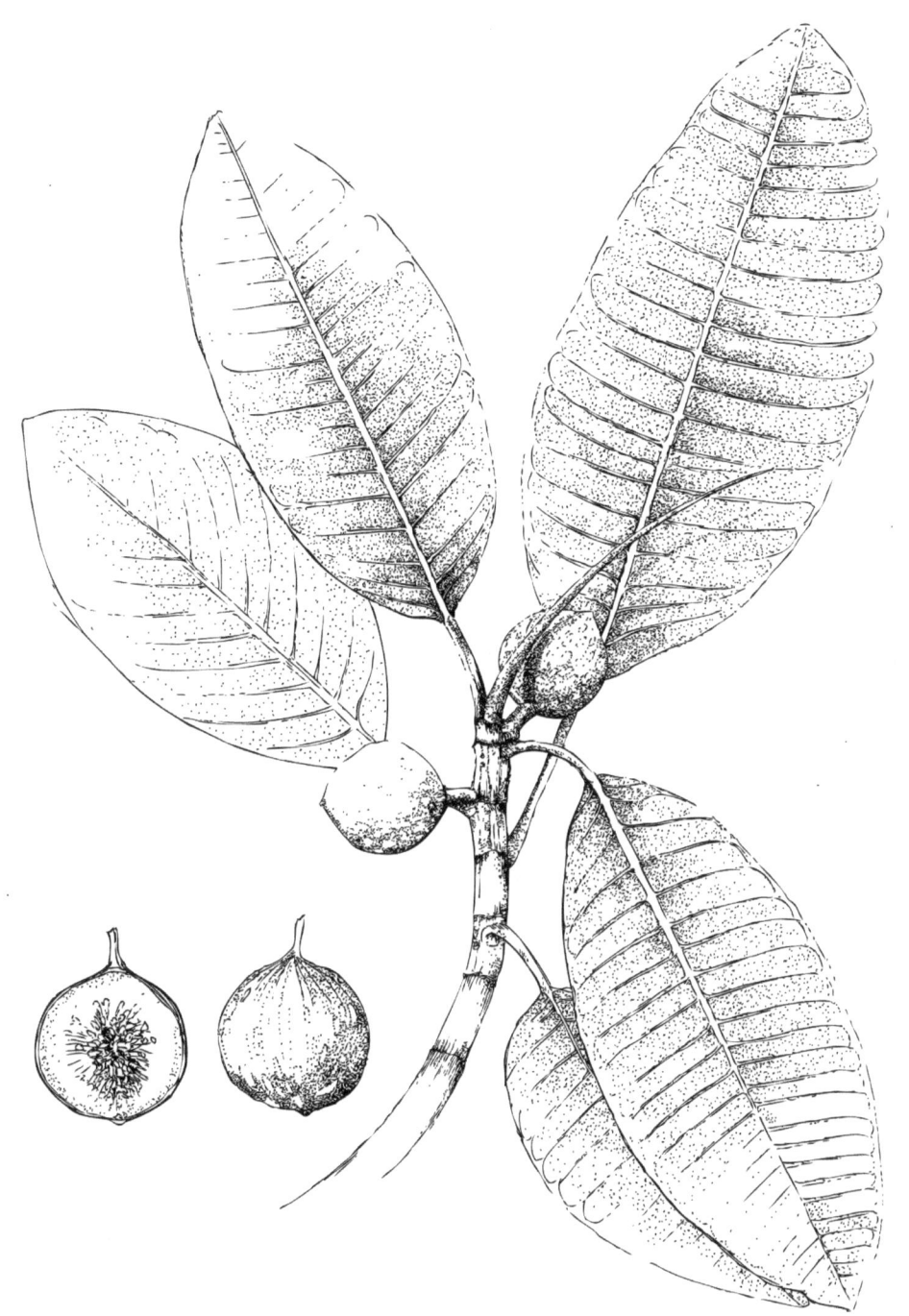

EIGHTEEN

The Cure for Drunkards

They say the best remedy for drunkards is the woman's placenta. You cut a little piece off, macerate it in alcohol and make them drink that. That will take the urge from you.

There's this centipede with a tough shell. Grab three of those and macerate them in alcohol. Bury it for one or two months. Keep it there buried, and then your maceration is ready. The alcohol makes the shell come apart in pieces but if it doesn't, you have to strain it and there's your remedy. You give that to the drunk without him knowing. You're going to trick them into drinking it, just three glasses. Don't give them any more than that, and it's done.

I cured my son with that even. He was a bad drunk. One time, it was carnavales and he comes home trashed. He had been in a fight with my other son. The other one, sober, kicked him twice and that laid him out on the floor. He's sitting there, and I tell some guy, Miguelín, "Go and find this."

The remedy, right?

"Paisa, paisa," Miguelin says to him.

"What's up?"

My son was wasted.

"Do you want to have a drink?"

"Bring it on, dammit."

A little while later.

"Paisa, have another one."

← Species of centipedes used medicinally, for drunkards (above) and for love spells (below)

We continue chatting, pretending we're drinking, "Paisa, another drink?"

"Alright then goddamnit, pass it to me," he says to him.

That's why he's no longer like that; he was cured. He was the worst drunk, the big guy. He drank and drank and fell asleep. That's that centipede's power.

Then there was this lady too. Her son was a drunkard.

She asks me, "Hey Duri, don't you know a cure for drunks?"

"Of course," I tell her. "There is one on your farm, ma'am; there are these bugs."

"Which one is it though?" she says to me.

"That centipede, I'm sure you have those on your farm," I tell her. It was in the bajíos, right?

"Yes," she tells me. "There are that kind."

"Macerate three of them, bury them for a month," I told her. "And you give him that without him realizing it."

Now the man no longer drinks. He was cured.

There are black and yellow ones—they're also for getting women. That bug has a habit of drying out. You grab its shell, rub it well and wipe it on your face. Then you walk behind the girl you want and you throw yourself into the bushes. By the afternoon already she'll be with you.

All of these little things I understand, but I don't like doing them. I've learned but I haven't touched them.

Shihuahuaco fruits (*Dipteryx micrantha*) →

NINETEEN

Shihuahuaco

I've healed people without taking ayahuasca. Drinking ayahuasca though, I learned more. But you shouldn't present yourself as someone who knows... No.

When you see a little boy or girl that has had harm done to them, you look at them and say to their mother, their father, "I'm a doctor."

That's all you say to them. You blow tobacco on the crown of their little head, their chest, their back. With that one treatment, if they get better, they'll say, "That one knows," and they'll tell other people. Never boast about what you know. This science isn't about charging money. See, a voluntary contribution is all you can receive.

You have to have your *cachimbo*,[132] your wooden pipe. Here, we make them from shihuahuaco.[133] It's a powerful tree, strong. You must cook that wood in the pot with ayahuasca, three times. Then fill it with tobacco and blow your smoke three times on the person you're going to heal. You have to inhale and puff and then it will get you drunk, that pipe, and when you're already a bit dizzy, that's when you heal.

When you drink the bark of the shihuahuaco, you can hear the sound of wind coming. That's the strength of the shihuahuaco, wind is its power. For defense too, it scatters off all the hoodlums milling about around you.

---

132. Ceremonial pipe.
133. Tree. *Dipteryx micrantha* (Fabaceae). Also commonly spelled chihuahuaco.

Shihuahuaco is good for improving your strength. It is also taken to fortify the blood. From the center of the trunk comes something like chicha.[134] You have to cut it down to drink that. Man, it's delicious. You can store that chicha once you've collected it and drink it whenever you want. Its color looks like water with brown sugar, but it's very hard to get the water from that one around here. When the trees are healthy they produce it, but there aren't any near here.[135]

---

134. Some shihuahuaco trees have a central cavity with a liquid inside of it, called chicha, as it is thought to be fermented and aged within the tree trunk.

135. Due to deforestation for its fine timber and for charcoal making, shihuahuaco is no longer found in the forests immediately adjacent to the village center of Infierno.

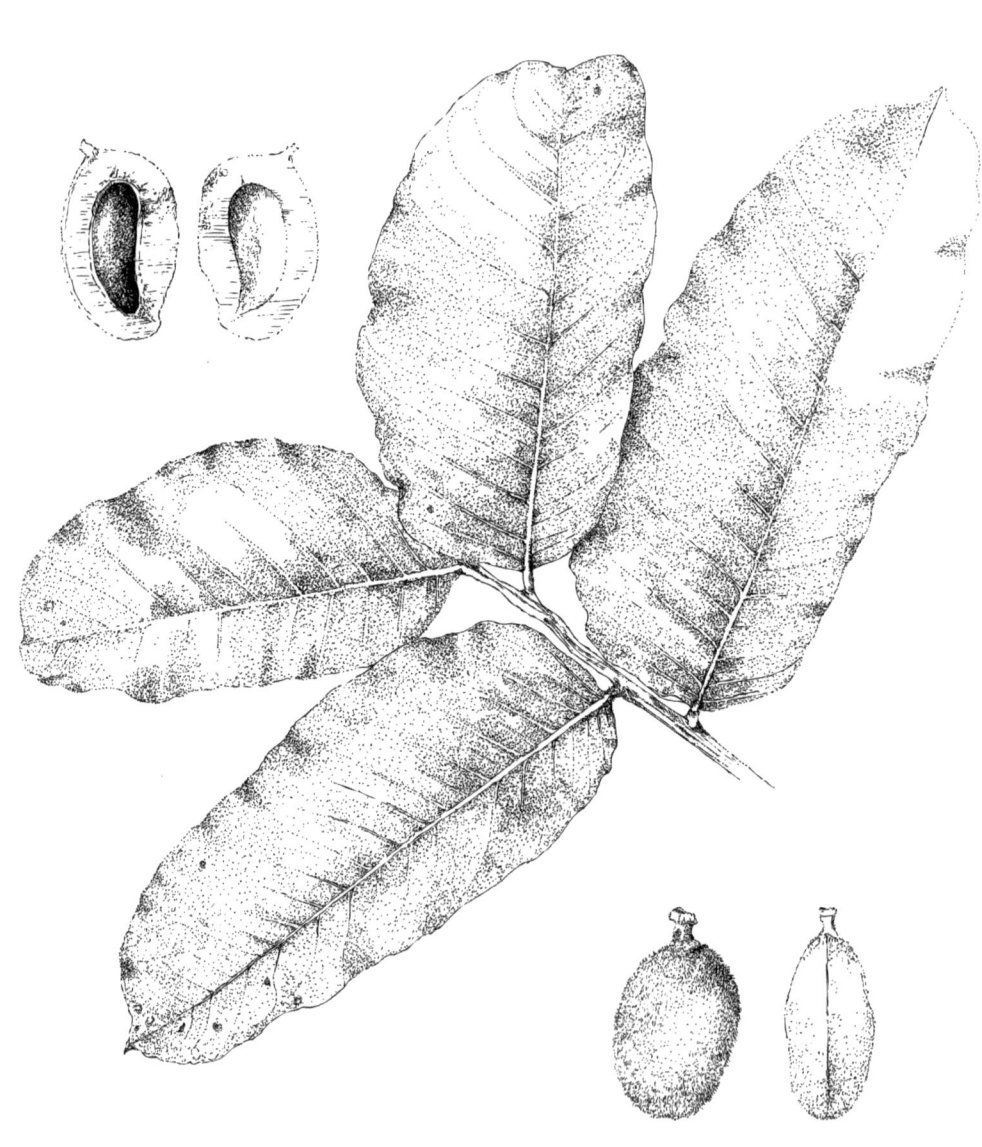

TWENTY

The Brazilian Spiritualist and His Cachimbo

Once, they took me to harvest Brazil nuts on the Piedras River. I worked there with a Brazilian who was a spiritualist.[136] He had all types of powders and he had his cachimbo, his pipe. It was enormous, like this, and he called it Gato Preto. It had the figure of a mermaid coming out of the water and another entering the water, drawn on his pipe. He was going to heal a woman.

There were about eight of us. With just his pipe, making all of them smoke, he made them all drunk with tobacco and I don't know what else. I guess he put plants in there. Geeze, just like with ayahuasca it made them purge. For me, the only thing I heard was that it made some hens fight, the hens fighting, just that, some noisy parrots cackling over there. There's a little partridge that goes "*crah craah craaah craaah*." Yanayuto they call it, because it's black.[137] The Brazilian was making all that happen.

Sure, but I didn't get drunk, I just heard all that. We were there until one in the morning. That's when we fell asleep. What I heard there, the hens, the chickens, the ducks, I've never seen that. I've never heard that ever again. The next day, I'm on my way

---

136. *Espiritistas* and *oracionistas* are kinds of healers who heal through prayer, as opposed to ayahuasqueros who heal using ayahuasca.
137. Because *yana* means black in Quechua.

← Shihuahuaco (*Dipteryx micrantha*)

141

to bathe myself, to wash myself in the stream. I bump into the Brazilian there, and he asks me:

"*Patrício*,[138] how was it with Gato Preto?"

"*Não, patrício*," I tell him, "*Gato Preto não presta para mim.*" (Gato Preto doesn't work for me.)

"No, patrício, you know something else," he says to me.

Well, he had seen.

"Why don't you take puré?"[139]

It's an aquatic plant. It's from the water, that one, but here we call it *tarope*. Over there in Manuripi, there's a lot of it on the rivers. You part them with your canoe and then they close back again behind you. That's what that plant is like, it's aquatic.

"You only have a little further to go to become a different person," he tells me. "You should take puré, keeping the diet three months. Then you can enter the water, you can sleep there. You want to go to the other side of the stream, and in the river there's a plant that grows long, like this. You grab your machete, throw the plant in the river and you can pass across there as if there was a bridge."

That's what the Brazilian told me.

In the lakes, on the shores, there's this herb that's aquatic. It grows on the water. It has a round leaf and its fruit looks like a little pineapple. They call it tarope here, and in Brazil they call it puré. Boil that and drink it. *Oof*, it will teach you in the best way. Mix it with a little bit of tobacco. Boil it with that, drink some

---

138. Brazilian Portuguese equivalent of *paisano*, word meaning fellow countryman, compatriot, from the same country or land.

139. In this story, Don Ignacio could possibly be referring to water hyacinth, the aquatic plant *Eichhornia crassipes* (Ponthederiaceae), which in some parts of Brazil is known as *aguapé* or *aguapey*, among other common names. Researching the plants mentioned by Don Ignacio in his stories, no ethnographic record could be confirmed for a plant called puré, nor called by the common name tarope; but this lack of information about common names used by different ethnic groups and in different regions is prevalent with regard to plants of the Amazon.

of it, and in your dream that one will teach you. It's a wonderful plant.

I've taken that plant only once, for defense. Man, it's nice. Other ayahuasqueros chase after you, and *boom!* You jump in the water. You're sleeping underwater and they're looking for you outside. They were coming after me like that. I entered the water and slept inside a hollow log; that's where I would go. And a man from the highlands was waiting for me outside. He wanted to steal what I knew, and when I came out of there, we started beating each other up. We hit each other, fighting. I chased him off so he wouldn't take away my power.

That plant is good, it's for defense. Some joker comes in to tug at you and there you are, in the water. Twice it's defended me. I've never taken it again since. Here, there isn't any, you see. I've searched for it at Lake Sandoval, I've looked for it in Tres Chimbadas,[140] and there isn't any. Wherever people go, it disappears. Then there isn't any. Its flower is purple; it's pretty. It must be a remedy for women too—purple flowers are for getting women. Here, where we go fishing, there is some, but it's different. I want to bring some to see how it works. It's boiled together with ayahuasca.

There are lots of things to heal yourself with. We just don't know them, right? And it's hard for other ayahuasqueros to knock down someone who knows herbs, because you have the power of the plants with you. And he who doesn't know herbs, he can be knocked down in a second.

---

140. Sizeable oxbow lakes near the Madre de Dios and Tambopata Rivers, respectively.

TWENTY-ONE

Vision

You don't see all the time. There are times when you see very clearly. You drink and you see. But there are times when you only see little things, and there are times when you only see colors. I wonder what it depends on? The vine, the plant itself doesn't want to teach you, I guess.

They're forest spirits, the ones you see. In this science, they look after me. All I see is people dressed in white.

"That's the army that's looking after you."

They've told me they're from ayahuasca, an army of people dressed in all white that are the offspring of ayahuasca, ayahuasca's people.

When people don't have any visions with the plant, why might that be? Well, the plant doesn't want to teach them either. Sometimes it's like that. It doesn't want to teach you because if you're going to learn, you might turn evil. That's why it doesn't teach you. Bad people, people who… anyway, who knows what they do with their lives? You see them in the shape of pigs, as swine, like dogs, or in the shape of cats. Those aren't good folks. The people that you see that way are real pieces of work.

Do you think others will tell you what I'm telling you? They're pieces of work. They want to be the only ones to learn. I call them out about that. A person should talk about what they've seen, what they know. Right? Some don't, though. They're selfish. There's no way they'll talk to you. They don't want you to see the

← Water Hyacinth flower (*Eichhornia crassipes*)

145

monkey business they're up to. You watch them too. From down below, they turn off the lights; they take your vision away.

For example, you're drunk, you're watching me. I've already seen you and so I work you where you can't see me, slowly, until you no longer see. The lights went out and you don't see me anymore and I just go about my life, because they watch everything, you know, they see everything.

In order to see, you have to hit tobacco hard nine times. You have to take three drags of smoke and blow it out forcefully. Then you smoke again, exhale again, nine times. Then your sight clears up. That's its secret, but you have to hit it hard, inhale the tobacco deep. Up high, you can see plants for snakebite, against scorpion stings, bullet ant[141] stings.

In my drunkenness, I've seen that he who drinks ayahuasca hardly ever runs into snakes. They're afraid of you. I wonder what power the body has, eh? In my drunkenness, I've seen that when you're walking along, they all run off—spiders, crickets, snakes, all sorts. There's a song of the forest. It's Chullachaqui's.[142] That song, when you sing it to go out into the forest, you don't find anything, no animal will get close to you. It's as if you're singing an ícaro. Chullachaqui is afraid of me, that fool. What, you think he's going to show himself to me?

The animals that appear in visions are there to see if you can handle seeing those animals. If you're afraid of that animal, you can't learn, you're a coward. It makes you sit as if you're on the edge of a cliff. You're looking; it seems like you're going to fall. If you got frightened, you're not going to learn.

One time, a man took me some place. We had a ceremony there with another guy and we drank.

"Hey Duri," he tells me—we were right at the height of our drunkenness—"my compadre has lost something. Let's see if you can review the case."

---

141. *Paraponera clavata*, locally known as isula.
142. A forest spirit whose name can be translated as Odd Foot, known for tricking people into getting lost in the forest.

He had lost I don't know what; he didn't tell me what. He said he couldn't see it. That's all he said.

"Alright," I tell him.

Bernardino was the guy's name.

"Don Bernacho," I say to him.

"What do you say, maestro?"

"Let's see. I'll sing a *huayno*[143] and you'll see it."

I started to sing. I sang to him and it all presented itself: the guy appeared, two guys, over there in that big stream across the river. They were up there.

"Look," I say to him, "up there on the bank of the stream, he lives there on the other side. On the bank of the stream, they're carrying a pig. I'm not sure what they're dragging along," I told him, "Can you view it?"

"No, I can't see."

"There they are. There are two of them," I said to him.

I didn't know what it was all about. On the stream's bank, two people are looking at a bulky shape, then they're carrying a pig, dragging it along. I'm not sure what I was looking at. And I tell the man, "There's a little path over there, along the side of the stream. They're carrying a pig along that way. I'm not sure if it's a pig. It looks like a pig."

That's what I was seeing in the vision.

"Alright, maestro," he tells me.

So, that happened, and the following day I came back and, well, the man already knew…. And it was true, they had stolen a cow and a fishing net of his from the big stream. The fishing net had been left set in the stream, you see.

On the stream, on the other side, on that high ground is where they lived. The guy arrives, the owner of the animal, and looks at the path and sees his cow's tracks and he follows them. He gets closer to see and it turns out they hadn't taken the animal's hide; they hadn't even hidden it. The hide was lying on the bank of the

———

143. An Andean folk song of a particular rhythm.

stream. They had killed it on the flat bottoms down by the stream bed. And there were a bunch of vultures all gathered there. He goes to have a look. They had butchered the cow the day before. It was a large cow, see. And there, covered with leaves, were the head and the hide. Then he left there.

He went up—those people's house was located on the high ground. He called out a greeting.

"Is there something I can help you with, Don Bernardino?"[144] they say.

"I've come to see about an issue with something that has slipped away from me. It seems like you've grabbed it."

"No, Don Bernardino. What would I steal?"

"No, I already know. You've got it."

He had already seen the cow hide, right?

"Yes," he says to him, "I've taken your fishing net, but I didn't take it by myself. Here it is."

Just like what I saw, you see, between the two of them they were carrying a bulky object. He pulled the fishing net out of a sack and handed it over to him. Then the man said to him, "But I've come about another issue, not about this."

"What's that then? I haven't seen that."

"No, you can't deny it," he gets straight to the point. "I've seen it. You can't deny it." Geeze, that shut the guy right up.

"Alright, Don Bernardino. I've slaughtered your cow. Now, what do you want? Do you want me to give it back to you or pay you?"

"Give me back another cow."

His pastureland was over there on the other side. A tiny stream divided the pasture in two. They rounded up the cow between the two of them and the old man also picked up his fishing net.

---

144. Don Ignacio seems to forget that, earlier in the story, it was Bernardino's compadre who was the owner of the cow. But probably Bernardino claimed it was his compadre's loss in order to save face, when it was actually his.

He called for me again after that. I went there. Heck, he says to me, "What you told me is exactly what happened. I want to make you a proposal. I'll give you four cows and a bull. Raise them and keep half the earnings. Over there in Infierno nobody raises cattle. Make your ranch," he says to me.

I told my children about it, but they rejected the offer.

Plant without a common name
Ombrophytum sp. (Balanophoraceae)

There's a little plant that comes up from the soil looking like a sort of ear of corn. It resembles a penis. It's red and looks like the scales of the aguaje fruit. You have to pull it out carefully; it's a tuber, like this big. Its root emerges from there. Its vine is thick. It has everything you have, complete; it has everything a woman has too. You have to grate that, macerate it in alcohol and drink it. They say it's potent. I can't find it. I knew it grew around here; I've gone to look for it. The rainy season is when it comes out, see, and I haven't been going out into the forest for a while. That's for the man that's not functioning properly.

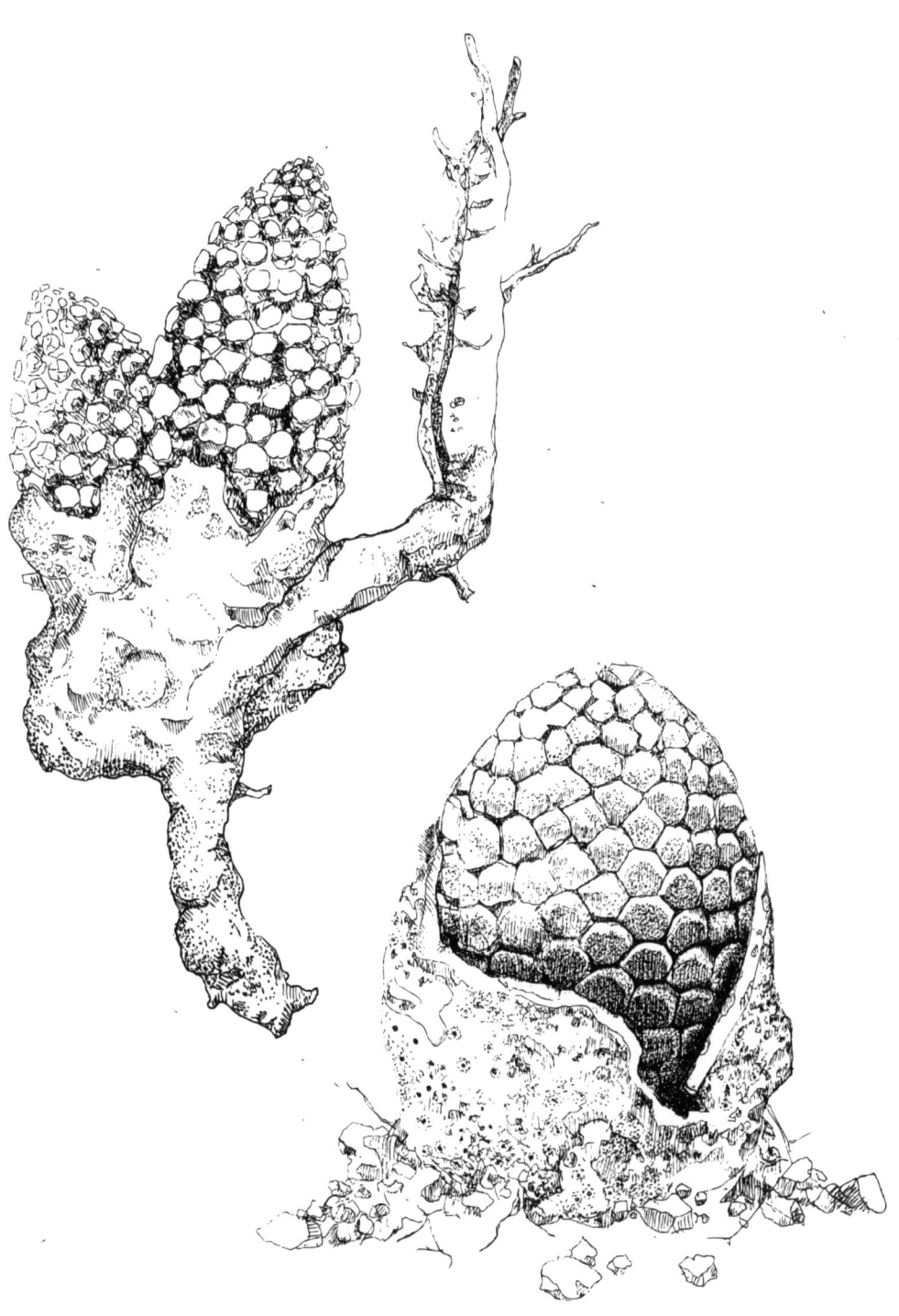

Patiquina
Diefenbachia sp. (Araceae)

Patiquina is for defense. You bathe yourself with it. It burns, that one. The brujos watching you will see that you're burning and that's why they won't be able to do anything to you.

To give a steam bath to those that have had harm done to them by brujos, you use patiquina, catahua, tangarana and pucunaucho hot pepper:[145] a steam bath. Let the bastard defend himself if he knows how. I make people bathe themselves. That's why the brujos can't see me.

The strength of patiquina is fire; tangarana has ants and gives you a fever; catahua is active poison; and pucunaucho pepper burns. Of those four things, a kilo each—you boil it and the person receives its steam. And the one that did the harm, may he defend himself if he knows how, because if not they'll get a stomach pain and at four in the morning it's all over. It's violent, that's why I don't like that one.

Palo de Agua
Meliosma herbertii (Sabiaceae)

Palo de agua is for the liver. It's like drinking unsweetened coffee. You grate it, boil water and just infuse it in that, then you strain it and store it. If you get bitten by a bullet ant, you grate it and stick that on, and it won't hurt.

Para Para →
Abuta grandifolia (Menispermaceae)

Para para is for erectile dysfunction, but you have to add another ingredient, see. You have to prepare it with honey. Just drink one cup every morning or before going to bed, and you'll wake up hard as a rock.

---

145. Tangarana is *Triplaris* sp. (family Polygonaceae) and ají pucunaucho is a popular local variety of *Capsicum chinense* (Solanaceae).

Pipa →
Macrolobium acacifolium (Fabaceae)

Pipa is good for internal wounds; correction of the blood; to clean the blood; for multiple internal wounds. It's good for all that. It helps wounds close. It's one for women, especially for cancers that only affect women.

The diet for pipa is to eat normally, you just don't eat beef or pork, and the most important thing to diet is sex. You wake up in your bed in the early hours of the morning and take a sip, at lunch time, before eating, and another one before going to bed in the evening—three a day until you finish the bottle. If you want to finish in a year, take it for a year. If you want to finish right then, you take it all at once so you don't have to take it any more [laughs].

Piquito de Varoncito
unidentified species

Fruit like a little penis, use it to have only male children. Before getting pregnant, the woman should play with the fruit or use it as a necklace.

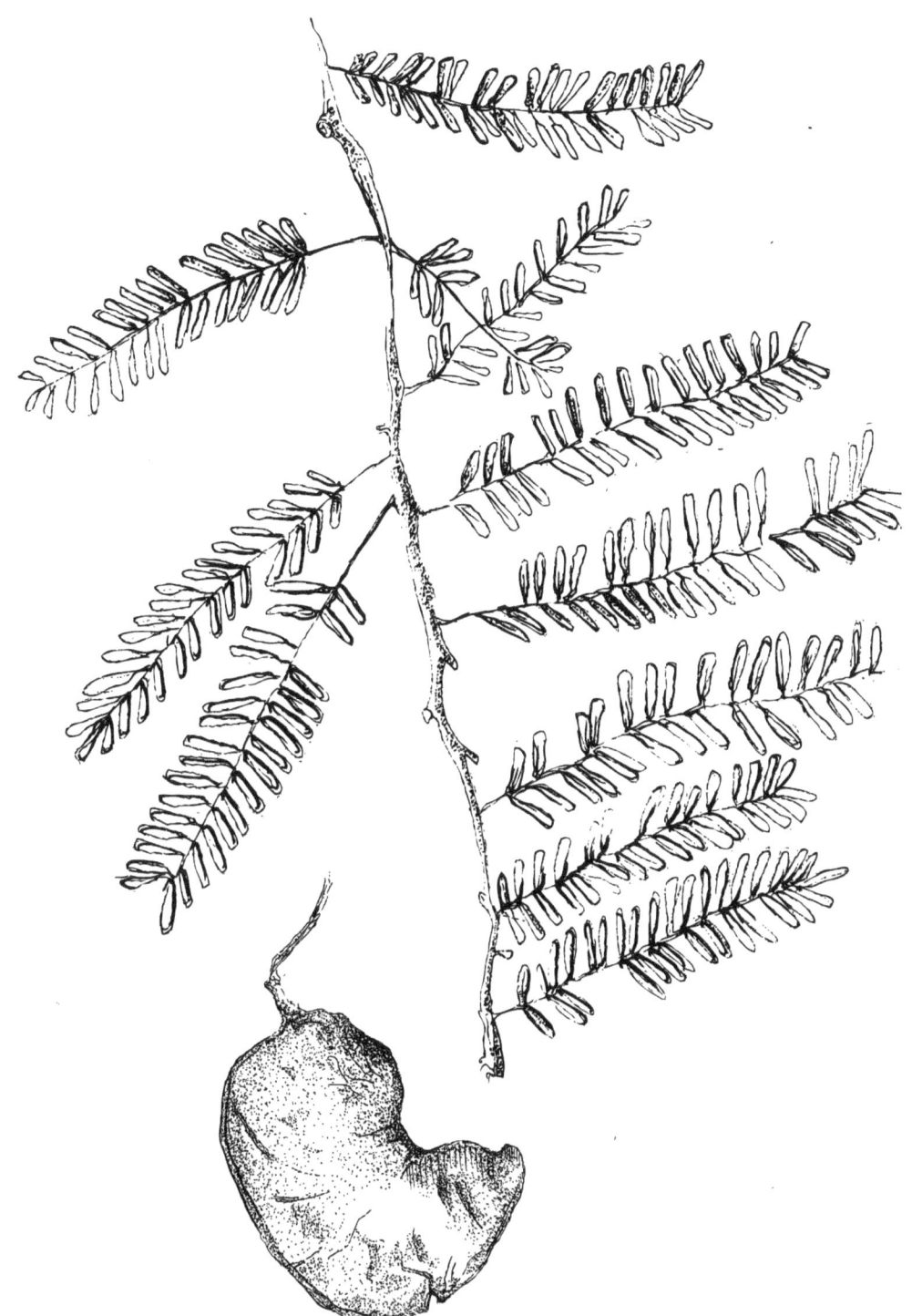

The Renacos[146] *Ficus* sp. (Moraceae)

Renaco

The resin of renaco is good for poultices, for fractures, sprains. You can take it too, but you have to mix it with another bark to make it more potent.

Renaco Warmi

The underside of the leaf is the same color as the red howler monkey.[147] It's good for kidney pains, female pains, when their vagina hurts. For women's fractures, stick the resin on as a poultice.

Matapalo or Renaquilla

Just raw like that, not too much, just one little cup is what you have to bleed from it. You drink that while you're dieting and it'll go down better than eating a plantain. That plant is for people suffering from anemia, for those that are thin, for dysentery, for all those things. Its leaf is big, like this.

Camel

It's a long liana, a type of renaco. Its leaf is round like this, double thickness. Its liana grows very straight, taut. When you want to learn from this one, you look for the youngest part of its root. Boil a small piece of it with ayahuasca and you'll learn. It'll teach you everything, put in just two or three pieces. It's really good for defense too. When your enemies come: boom, you climb up to the heights. The person that doesn't know about this plant and is following you—you're already above them, up top.

---

146. Renaco is a local term for most or all of the many species from the genus *Ficus* in the Peruvian Amazon, and especially for strangler figs. This is a genus of disproportionate frequency and importance in Amazonian forests.
147. In Peru, coto, red howler monkey. *Alouatta sp.*

Renaco (*Ficus* sp.), various species →

Sacha Picuro
Alternanthera sp. (Amaranthaceae)

This is an herb to cure dogs; sacha picuro is its name, I think. Its root is like a carrot. To cure dogs, to make them good paca hunting dogs, give them the grated root in a broth of the very same paca. Then the dog won't sit still when you cure it with that. I want to give it to my little dog, my Chota. Also, for snake bite, grate it and drink that herb.

Sangapilla →
Chamaedorea angustisecta (Arecaceae)

Right now this flower is ready to be turned into a remedy. You have to macerate it in sugar cane alcohol. For stomach cramps, that's the strength of this little plant.

Surucuina
Eclipta prostrata (Asteraceae)

Surucuina is another remedy for snakes. It has a large root. You grate that and in a piece of cloth, you add water to the little pieces, you wring it out and that's what you drink.

TWENTY-TWO

The Plant that Heals

There was a teacher here who was from Urubamba, and he came here to the community with his little lady. The wife was from Pucallpa, an older woman. The man was a bad drunk; he hit his wife for absolutely no reason at all.

And a guy calls me from down the way. He comes and he says, "Hey Duri! This is what's going on, dammit. I want to drink ayahuasca."

Alright then, I went and I fetched the ayahuasca. In those days, they used to teach all day, and the teacher gets out of work at like 5 o'clock in the afternoon and stops by.

"So, *cumpa*,[148]" he says to me—he never addressed me by my name—"so cumpa, what are you up to?"

"I'm preparing the chicha, teach."

They already knew that I drank. He and his wife accompanied me to drink over there, down the way. We left at six in the afternoon.

We get there, the clock has struck eight in the evening, and we're drinking the chicha. The guy is here, across from me, the teacher next to him and the lady over there. And then, the teacher is already dizzy, the other guy too, and I ask the lady, "Ma'am, how are you? How are you feeling?"

"Nothing," she says to me. "I feel normal, Don Ignacio."

"Let's see, give me your hand," I say to her.

---

148. Short for *compadre*, used as a term of casual endearment between friends or acquaintances.

Why did I take her by the hand? Geeze, I held her hand and within five minutes the little lady was seeing all the way back to her birth. If a person doesn't get drunk, you hold their hand for just five minutes, darn it, and the drunkenness you have gets transferred to the person, see. Then you have to take more to accompany the person. It lasted until four in the morning, her drunkenness.

I looked the teacher over and it was as if he had a chimney coming out of his head: *boom!* Listen, he was completely under her thumb after that. His wife was in complete control. Ayahuasca cured him. That's why I'm too benevolent. I get money and I can't hold on to it.

I too consider it a drug, but it teaches you. You learn from this, right? And you learn to recognize the good people, the bad people. It teaches it all to you when you've dieted.

TWENTY-THREE

Remedies for Snake Bite

Snakes don't cause me any trouble. I've been bitten three times and they haven't harmed me at all. Only one of them made me swell up all red. I even fell asleep there in the forest.

The first time, it bit me here on my arm. I was clearing a farm patch, and there was one tree that I still had to cut down. I was going to cut its branches off, and when I went to chop it this colorful one was there, a loro machaco.[149] It had fallen from up in the tree. It had been coiled around a branch and *snap!* It got me, dang it. I looked at myself and there was blood coming out, and I looked at the snake. It was right there.

"Dad!" I called out.

"What's wrong?" he says.

"A snake bit me."

He called his brother. Norberto was his name.

"Norberto, Ignacio was bitten by a snake!"

They came to see. There it was. They killed it and split open its skull and took out its brains.[150] Since we had that Brazilian remedy,[151] they gave me that too, and in the afternoon, I was playing football as if nothing had happened.

---

149. Venomous snake. *Bothrops bilineatus* (Viperidae).
150. A popular secret to absorb the venom from a snake bite or insect sting, using the brains, entrails or meat of the same animal, placed on the affected area.
151. In the Peruvian Amazon, Brazilian anti-venom products of varying degrees of effectiveness are readily available for sale at markets and shops.

← Ayahuasca vine (*Banisteriopsis caapi*)

Then, it was when I was chasing after a monkey, because around there you have to chase down those sly monkeys.[152] There were two of us, and the monkey went into the brush, and I'm waiting for it to come out, and I was walking backwards and, *chomp*, it bit me here. "Geeze," I say, Nicasio was the guy's name, we were cousins-in-law. "Hey Nico, a snake bit me!" I tell him.

"Where, damnit?"

"Let's leave that monkey for now. Let's just go," I tell him.

We were an hour away from home. We left the monkey there and set off. I got there, still calm. They had a Brazilian remedy. They gave me that and I woke up fine.

Another time, I was bitten here when I was tapping rubber down on the Manuripi. I was working shiringa with this one guy and he had left to get some supplies. I tell him, "I'm going into the forest to find honey." There's tons there, see.

I went through a large aguajal swamp, but of the dense kind, like they have in Manuripi. The aguajales are quite big over there!

I found a beehive and got like three bottles of honey. At around three in the afternoon, I wanted to go back, but I didn't know where I'd come into it from or where to go to get out. I walked the whole day and couldn't get out. Damn, I said, where am I?

There are enormous aguajales in Manuripi! I wanted to cross that aguajal in order to exit it. I went to where the grass was. I started to take one step after another. With each step it got softer and softer, and a bit further down there was a massive boa track on top of the grass. So I said, "Shoot, I better not." I turned around. There are paths like that, leading into the lake. I guess they're from the prey that the wild beasts drag in, because there are lots of fierce beasts there! The animals that enter those lakes don't come back out again, see.

Before that, the snake had bit me. I had put its meat on the bite and I was limping along. At five I was soaked by a rain that fell, a really intense shower, dang it.

---

152. "Around there" in Bolivia, Ignacio implies, pressure from hunters meant that monkeys were less tame and thus harder to hunt.

And that forest is like a banana plantation. Since the wild plantain leaf is nice and big, I cut off some leaves.[153] There was a large renaco there with buttress roots.

"This is where I'm going to sleep, damn it all," I said to myself.

I stretched out between the buttress roots. I drove a stake into the ground there, tied the leaves to it nice and tight, and got myself situated in there. With my leg already all numb, I shut myself in and sucked down honey all night long.

My leg had swollen up fat. I couldn't walk, man! The next day, my leg was all red and swollen. It must have been that the honey was cutting the effect of the venom. I got up and started walking again, going round in circles in the aguajal; I didn't know where I'd come in.

At around two in the afternoon, I hear a shot like, *toom!* My friend was looking for me, see. I replied. I went slowly in that direction, dragging my leg along, all red and darn heavy. Then, a bit closer to me, he hit a tree trunk. I replied and he came over. He found me; the guy brought me food, thank goodness.

"Darn it, what's happened to you?"

"I'm screwed. I can't walk. I was bitten by a snake."

"Geeze! Shall I carry you?"

"No, let's just go like this."

He looked for itininga,[154] crushed it and stuck it on. We headed out, with me following him slowly behind. We came out into the rubber estrada when it was already dark. At seven, eight we arrived, carrying the rubber too. I was dragging my leg along; I couldn't walk, you see. The next day, he went to find a remedy and the bastard didn't come back for three days!

You can drink itininga too, and if you don't have any water, you have to drink it with your urine. Its leaf is like the leaf of the

153. Platanillo is a common name that refers to a variety of wild species that are closer or more distant relatives of the banana, with similarly long, broad leaves.

154. A hemiepiphyte, *Philodendron* sp. (Araceae), whose aerial roots are used as a remedy against snake bites.

uncucha,[155] like this big. But moronga[156] is even better. It's the same but in a longer vine. That one comes from higher up, it's all covered in little nubs and is strong like a wire. That one is also good against the bushmaster's bite. Find the freshest part of the shoot, measure three hand widths of it, cut it and chew it well after the snake has bitten you. Pound it thoroughly and apply it. If there isn't any water around, use the water from the water vine.[157] And if you can't find that, mix that little bit of crushed plant with your own urine and drink that, and stick the remains of what you chewed on the place where you were bitten. It won't swell at all nor hurt. It's really good, better than itininga. It burns.

Out of that one they make baskets too, from that plant. Here they don't utilize it but in Cobija[158] they make baskets out of it, there where I'm from. It also works for making women lose babies; it can be prepared for that too. Just mash two little pieces of itininga and give her that to drink. This plant works for snake bite and as an abortive for women.

I've seen them high up in my drunkenness. On those big trees there are these little plants that grow and their root is like an onion. That one's also good for snake bite. You mash three or four of those, drink it and stick it on the bite too. That's what I've been taught in my drunkenness.

---

155. A cultivated plant, *Xanthosoma sagittifolium* (Araceae), with heart-shaped leaves and an edible rhizome.

156. Another hemiepiphyte similar to itininga and of the same genus, *Philodendron* (Araceae), moronga is also used as a fixed fishing line of the kind that has multiple hooks attached.

157. The common names *soga de agua* ("water vine") or *soga maravilla* ("wonder vine") refer to several species of liana that provide abundant drinking water that runs freely from out the ends of the cut vine pieces.

158. Cobija, Bolivia, capital of the Pando department.

Aguaje (*Mauritia flexuosa*) →

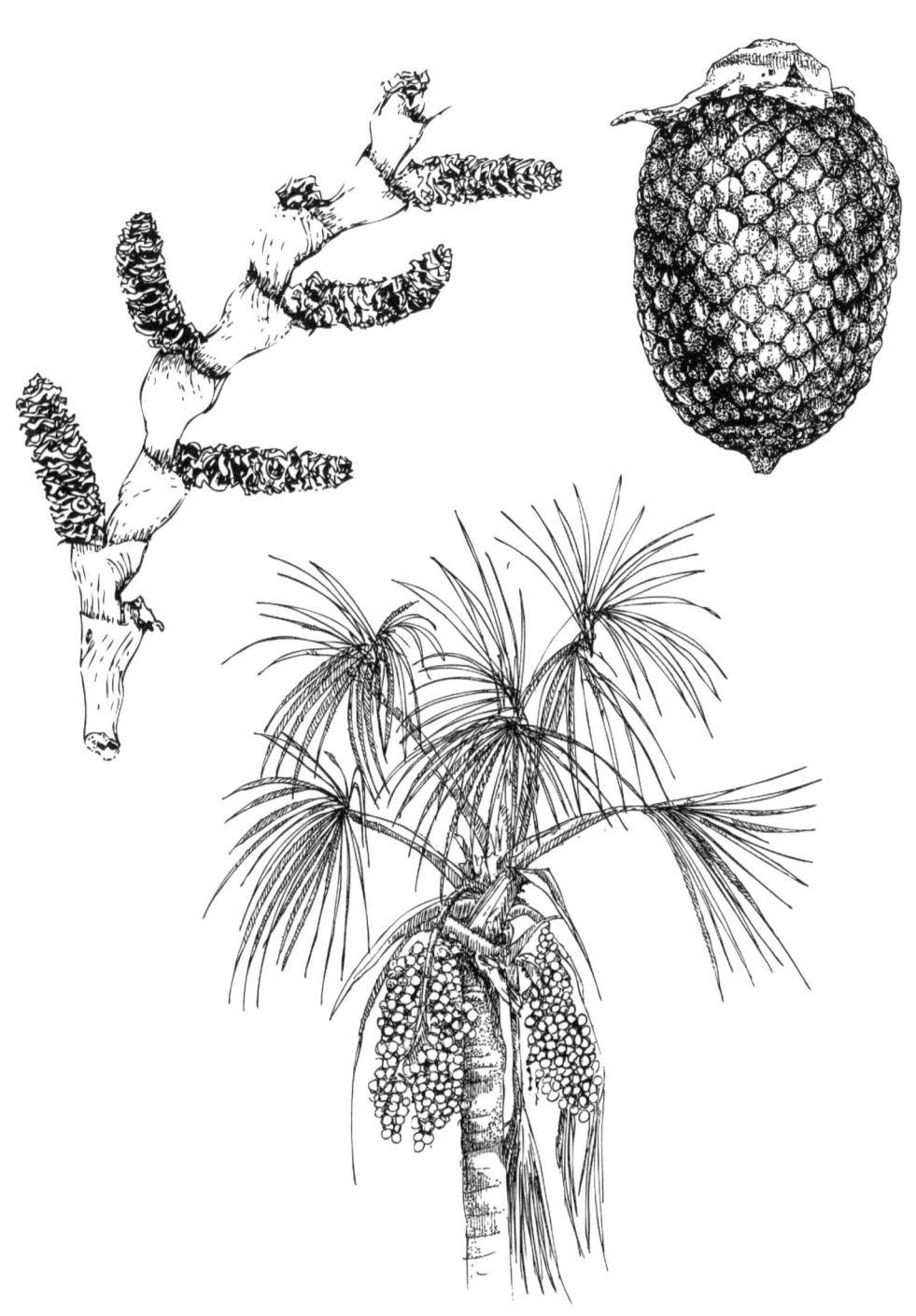

TWENTY-FOUR

The Bushmaster and the Boa

The oil of the bushmaster is for eyesight and for leishmaniasis. First, you have to clean the sore well, then put the oil all over the wound, and the next morning it'll be white. It'll look as if you've squeezed lemon juice on it.

I've cured one little lady with that. She had two huge sores, this big. It's a really good one; three treatments and the leishmaniasis is gone. It's potent, that one. They've also told me that you take its eye and pop it. They say it hurts like hell, but it'll clear your eyesight. Apply the "yolk" of its eye into your eye. It's good for your eyesight. They're one-of-a-kind remedies, those ones.

Bushmaster oil is very fatty; its fat is like a chain of little balls. You take it out, pop the little balls, put it all in a tin, let the sun melt it and then store it.

The head of the bushmaster is for defense, for when you have a lawsuit of some sort. You have to cut it carefully, though, dry it out and carefully cover it up in your left pocket. The idiot who's suing you won't know what to say, and justice will rule in your favor because the other person won't be able to speak. That's its power. Also, for evil eye,[159] see, you find a snakeskin, from any kind of snake. You lie down and you don't pick it up from the ground, just rub your eyes with it, you'll never get evil eye!

---

159. *Mal de ojo* or evil eye is a form of harm brought on by envy.

One time, they had killed a bushmaster while felling trees for a new farm patch around here. They cut it up and cooked it in pieces. They had put salt on it, but as a remedy you don't salt it. Its broth is white, but it smells delicious, like fish. I couldn't eat it. Later, I also killed one; I brought home a good-sized piece, I boiled it and again wasn't able to eat it. I haven't been able to find them anymore, I used to before, when I used to walk in the forest. I killed lots of bushmasters here. I used to walk into the forest at night; I can't go at night anymore. I used to go there with the mother of my children. I had a path over there that made a loop and popped out near here, and when I went with her, we were always lucky. That little lady had a good spirit. We would bring back deer, armadillos, paca. She'd bring back the small animals and I would carry the larger ones.

In the Bolivian jungle, when I was a young boy, with a friend, with another boy walking in the forest, I saw one a meter in height—that's how thick that bushmaster's body was. The jaguar had eaten it. I guess it had hunted it that night; it had put leaves all along its body, covering it. It was more or less ten meters long, but by then its body is no longer pretty.

I was twelve years old and the other guy was eighteen, I think. I carried a rifle, the other guy had a 16-gauge shotgun, and we had hunting dogs. We went into the jungle via some old rubber estrada paths. We suddenly heard the dogs go *Woof, woof!* and we said, "*Bushca!*"[160] He ran that way and I ran this way in a race to shoot first. It was a clear forest; in Bolivia there are some clear forests.[161] From afar, we managed to see it. There, under a palmiche,[162] there was a bushmaster piled up a meter high—but it's no longer pretty, a snake that size. We then saw how the jaguar was rolling around. Apparently the jaguar plays with it after he has

---

160. Typical alarm call to alert a hunting dog, from *busca*, or "Look for it."
161. *Monte libre* refers to a forest type with less dense understory vegetation, easier to walk through.
162. A dwarf palm tree used to thatch houses, from the genus Geonoma (Arecaceae).

killed it. And he had eaten a part of its neck, he had eaten its head and then left it covered up. We went and told the old man.

"Liars, how could there be a bushmaster that big?"

We took him to see it and it was true, there was the bushmaster. That bushmaster was a beast; I'd never seen anything like it. It's one thing to hear about it and another thing to see it for yourself.

One time the serpent ran me off. Up the La Torre River, there used to be a clay lick, and I was roaming around up there. I crossed one of those streams that's there right next to the La Torre, further upriver. It's a clear forest up there. I was checking out a lake, you see, a great big lake, wow, it was teeming with fish. I sat down on the trunk of a tree and here comes this snake they call the loro machaco. I saw it, dang, I got up and the bastard came right at me, so I slid around to the other side of the tree trunk and shot it. That's where I left the bastard. It made me run, man. That snake is a bad one.

In the Manuripi River, indeed, there are any number of boas, gosh darn it! There, on a beach, I've seen one that was a meter thick. It was coiled up in a pile. Its head was huge, like this big. That one will swallow you like a pill. I was there with a kid, and we went fishing. At Manuripi you catch nothing but spotted tiger catfish,[163] in no time at all. We went at like two in the afternoon. We got to the river by canoe along the shore, going down to the Manuripi. We were heading downstream. From afar we could see big bumblebees,[164] bees, butterflies, flies, all on top of it, making a noise. It was on a little beach; the beach was small, and the boa was lying there. It took up the whole beach. It must have been about twenty meters long.

"Hey, look at that boa," I say to him.

We got closer, up to a certain point.

"Hey, do I shoot it?" I said to him. I had a .22 rifle.

---

163. Doncella, a mid-sized fish, prized for eating. *Pseudoplatystoma punctifer* (family Pimelodidae).

164. The ronsapa is a type of large, aggressive bumblebee with a painful stinger.

"What an idiot you are! A bullet can't penetrate that one. Let's go. It could eat us," he says.

It was sunbathing there, that brute of an animal. That one doesn't even have to hit you anymore; it pulls you in like a magnet. You can't do anything to it then. If you shoot it and leave it there, it'll use its power to make you sick. We turned around, we left it there; it's probably still there now. What a gigantic boa! There are tons of boas, crocodiles there, enormous crocodiles! The boas are as common as earthworms there. I wonder how old they get? The cetico tree can grow from the back of the crocodile; it makes the tree walk around. One night it's here and the next night it's on the other side of the river. It walks around with herbs on its back. The herbs grow on it.[165]

At the mouth of the Malinowski, there's a stream that flows in. I went roaming around there once, and there are some of those clear paths that go into the forest.[166] I see a boa over there that's coming this way, foaming and lifting itself up. It was large, I'm guessing about a meter thick. Sheesh, what a brutal boa, a black one.[167] But it didn't see nor sense me, I'm sure. I was the only one to see it, walking alone as I was, and so I got the heck away from there. There's a deep pool in the main channel; that's where that one lives. It comes out of the pool and onto its little path. It looks like a canoe being pulled up onto land. This is how wide it is—what a giant boa! What, you think you're going to be able to kill it with a bullet?

---

165. As outlandish as Don Ignacio's claim may seem—that a tree can grow from the back of a caiman and be "walked around" by the caiman—in fact, cetico trees are often found in an epiphytic growth mode (growing on another plant). It is not uncommon to find a cetico's roots anchored into the folds and textures of a palm tree's trunk a meter or two above ground. Sightings are common of caimans, especially large, older ones, with small plants anchored into (growing from) the uneven textures of their backs.

166. The massive bodies of large boas and anacondas flatten and clear vegetation as they move through the forest or through wetland grasses, creating these (frightening) "paths that go into the forest."

167. *Boa negra* and *boa de agua* are synonyms for anaconda, which is indeed a mainly aquatic boa constrictor with black rings on its body.

My brother and I once killed a boa, but gosh, we weren't able to skin it! Its skin is stuck on like with glue, and it stinks! We left it there and we never killed another boa again. Some folks eat boa. I mean, it doesn't eat anything else than meat, right?

I met this old man. We were headed I don't know where, to saw wood, to the Madre de Dios River, I think; and they killed a boa this thick for the old man, and he cut off a log of it, this big. He was a cook—he had his own little separate cooking pot to cook with—and the width of the boa was just right for the pot! He cooked it thoroughly in there and ate it calmly, without blinking an eye. They say it's good to eat boa; they say that then your hair will never lose its dark color. Black boa is the best, its oil.

With my son, Sixto, once we were upriver from here, making a canoe.

"Hey, let's put up a shotgun snare,"[168] I say to him. "Maybe we'll kill a tapir,[169] to at least bring that home with us," I say to him.

We went and I put up the snare. At around ten at night the shotgun trap went off with a shot.

"The snare has gone off. Let's go and see," I say to him. And there was a little stream and a pool right there; we went along it. There was no animal. The bullet had gone into a tree trunk. It must have been a bat which made it shoot.

Then he tells me, "I'm thirsty, dad, I'm going to drink some water."

Luckily he looked carefully. He said the boa looked like a giant catfish,[170] but its head was very close in to the shore—it was all coiled up there.

"Daddy, daddy!" he says to me.

"What's up?"

"Come here, there's a catfish."

---

168. Shotgun *armadillo*: a sort of hunting trap which consists of bait, often banana or Brazil nut, a shotgun facing the bait, and a length of string tied to the trigger of the shotgun.

169. Sachavaca, or South American tapir. *Tapirus terrestris*.

170. The common name zúngaro refers to several Amazonian species of large freshwater catfish.

I came over and took a good look.

"Dang it, this is a boa! If you'd have gotten down to drink water, this bastard would have grabbed you," I told him.

There's a little palm tree that's like an iron rod. I sharpened it well and went around to the other side. It was in the pool, the boa is right there, damnit, and *swish!* I drove it in, pulled it out again, *swoosh*, pulled it out again, *swoosh!* I pierced it three times. By the fourth time I pierced it, darn it, shit!—it retreated. That beast has exceptional speed; that beast is very agile. That must be why it manages to grab animals.

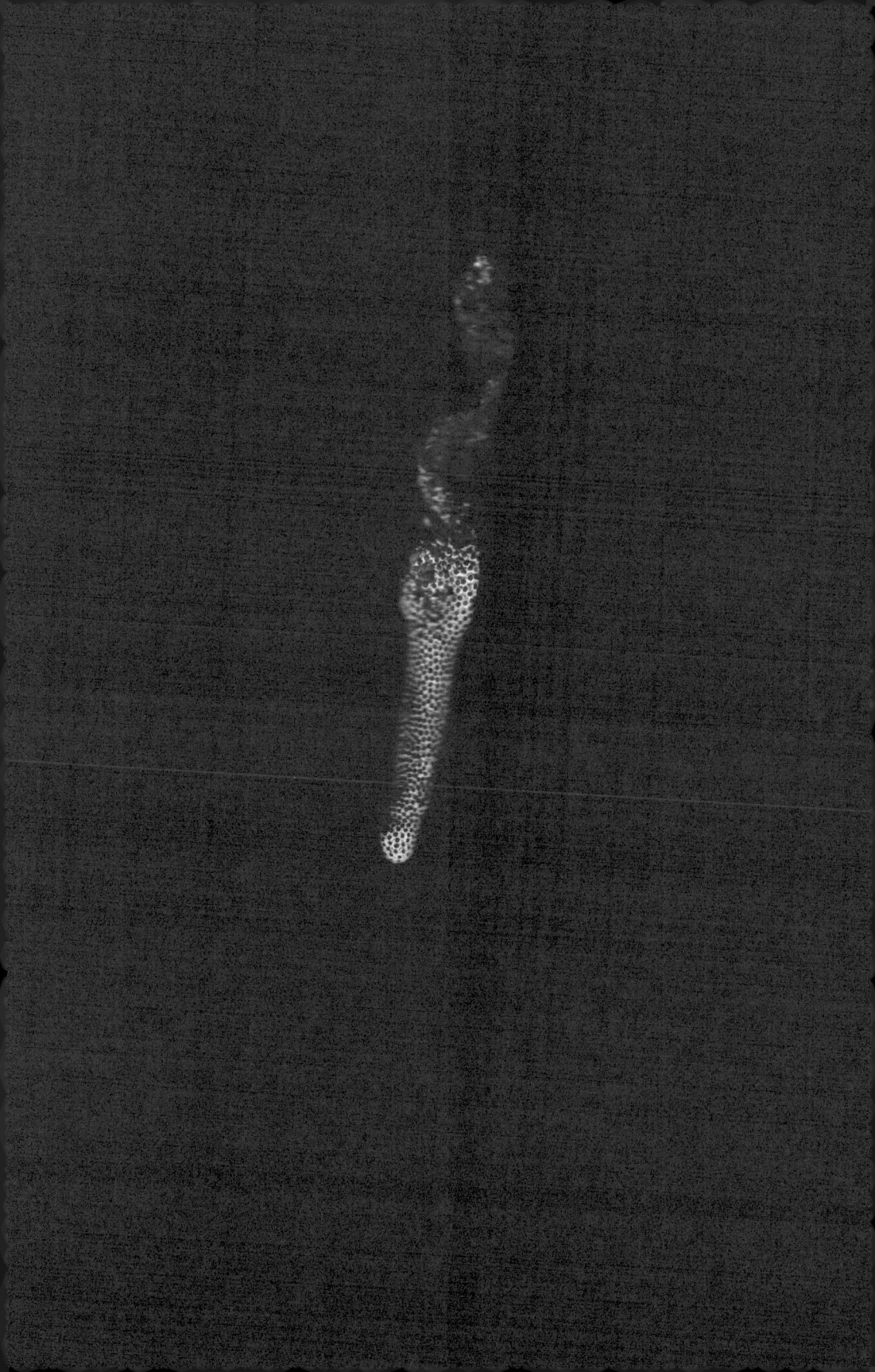

TWENTY-FIVE

The Woman, the Boa, and the Rubber Tapper

Once, there was this rubber tapper who got together with a girl and took her to the camp where he worked rubber, see. The girl was going to give birth to a baby boy.

The man, her husband, would go into the woods to tap rubber at the crack of dawn. She would make breakfast, calculating the time when he would be getting close by, and at around ten she would go following his same path, to collect the milk from the trees. She had a little dog, the girl. He would finish the tapping and then go catch up with her.

And one day, after he had finished tapping, he went to the spot where they would always meet up and she wasn't there. He went further along and he hears the little dog barking at the shore of the aguajal.

"I wonder what's going on there?" he said. "The dog must have found a jochi pintado."[171]

When the aguaje fruit is ripe, the boa waits there where the aguaje falls to grab prey. His rubber estrada reached the shore of an aguajal and the aguaje fruits were falling, you see. She went to pick them up and there was a boa there. She went to pick the

---

171. A common name used in Bolivia to refer to the edible rodent *Cuniculus paca* (picuro or majás in Perú).

← Cetico fruit (*Cecropia* sp.)

fruit up and the boa snatched the little lady and that's why the dog was barking.

It killed the woman; it swallowed her, see. Only her foot was sticking out of the boa's mouth. Gosh, and what did the guy do? The wife's husband, he slashed it with a machete. He split the boa open and took the little woman out. She didn't have any bones left, she was all crushed, looking like a rag. He brought her home like that, carried her like an animal. He arrived home, went to tell his co-worker, and they had a wake and buried her. The boa had swallowed her whole. That's why they say that on the shore of the aguajal, where it's clear, you have to be careful. The boa jumps quite far and will pull you in without any effort. It's dangerous there, where the aguaje falls at the water's edge. That's where that beast is, she's right there by the edge, waiting.

Manchinga fruits (*Brosimum alicastrum*) →

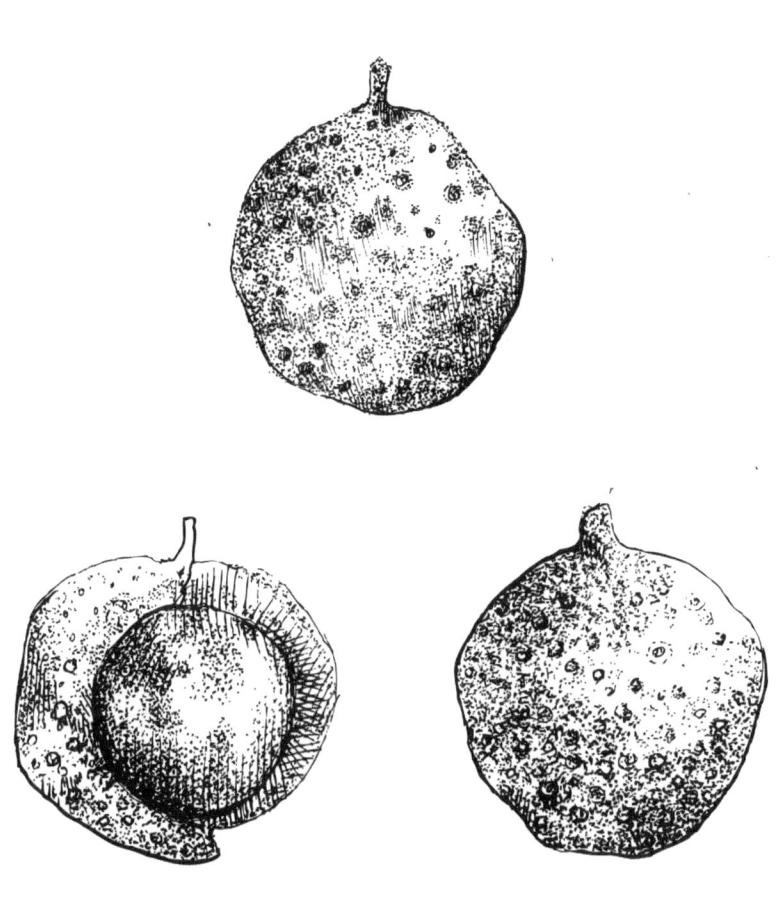

TWENTY-SIX

Hunting

I once went to work timber over at kilometer 172 with my brother. The road had already been built to as far at that point, there on the slopes of the foothills—beautiful hills.[172] We would fell a tree, get it situated properly, and cut the wood right there. Then, when we were coming back from there, from the slopes of the foothills, we came back by foot. There were no cars in those days, nothing like that.

The first car that came here by road was a certain man's, called Víctor, and his car was called Icebreaker, the first car to come here. It took over a month to get here, you see. The soil was soft. They would get stuck in the muck. They had to lay down leaves, branches, to get through. When the road was good, the car could drive fine. They took over a month, they say.

On the way back from there with my brother, there was a man, Carlos Salazar, with a hundred and sixty men with shovels. We stayed there for ten days, I think; the guy got us to stick around up there, since he knew me.

My brother and I, we would go into the forest. Tame spider monkeys,[173] collared peccaries, we brought back all kinds. He had four camps and at each of the four camps there were two designated hunters. We were only for one camp. That man knew how to manage people.

---

172. Don Ignacio refers to the road from Puerto Maldonado to Cusco, the Madre de Dios region's first land access route, completed in 1963. The foothills in question are the easternmost flank of the Andes.
173. Maquisapa, Peruvian spider monkey. *Ateles chamek.*

We worked only as hunters, you see. At this time of day, we would already be in the forest firing shots at the animals. We stopped for a bit, had breakfast at ten, and at around midday, we would go out again and bring home another batch. The cook would struggle. She had a helper to singe the monkeys; she skinned the monkeys and then would pass them to her helper. Collared peccaries, white-lipped peccaries, we would bring all of those. We found a feeding place. Oh, there were all sorts of animals in that clay lick—monkeys, we would kill all sorts of monkeys there. There would be a tapir standing there, collared peccaries, deer; we killed them there. We used to bring the animals back broken down, because you can hardly carry them in one piece. We would bring them broken down into pieces and already skinned, in a sack. Sometimes we would bring three deer each, chopped up in sacks. We brought everything, we didn't throw anything away. We were there for like ten or fifteen days. That man didn't want to let us go.

Going up into the hills there, you mimic the spider monkeys, they respond to you over here, over there. I went there in the year '72 by a footpath, along a stream. The tapir goes up that way. I wonder where it crosses over to? At around ten I think, I got to the top. I mimicked the spider monkeys there. I'm there, sitting on a tree trunk, on one little fin, I sat on a buttress root. The trees are low there, right?[174] Damn, they come from over there, from over here, within no time, it starts to fill up with a ton of spider monkeys. I choose the biggest one, the one that didn't have any young. I fire a shot at a great big one, *bam!* How those spider monkeys scream! They've never seen people. They were watching and got enraged. Now, to carry that big monkey. I just dragged it behind me.

I've been using a shotgun since I was nine, when I was still in Bolivia. That's why I don't really like to cook or wash my clothes. At this time of day, there's no way I'd be around the house! I was

---

174. The trees at higher elevation do not grow as tall as in the lowland forest.

listening to the agouti.[175] There are tons, just tons of them in Bolivia. I was sitting there, listening to the agoutis. I would kill two, three agoutis and come home.

I once killed two white-lipped peccaries; the peccaries are big over there. I was twelve by then I think. I disemboweled the two peccaries, I tied them up, one with its head facing this way, the other facing that way. I carried them like from here to the path over there, maybe fifty meters, then I'd put them down, only to pick them up again. I think I killed them at ten but I arrived with the two peccaries at six in the afternoon! Happy to arrive, you know? And that night I broke out in a fever. It affected my lungs. My dad then sent me to a place called Filadelfia where there was a German doctor. I stayed there for a month and got better. I don't have any trouble from it now. Damn, I struggled to get back, but I got back.

At night, over there in Bolivia, there's this biggish partridge; it lives there in the clear forest areas. I would sit down there quietly, and with a shotgun at that. I would be sitting there, I would calculate well, I'd shine a light… and there it was, with its white breast, and *bang!* Then I would come sit down again to calculate my aim two more times. That's how I killed as many as four, five partridges that I'd bring back with me.

Sometimes I would find that one kind of armadillo; they're enormous over there, the quirquinchos.[176] I would kill it and carry back its full weight. That's why my mother and the man who raised me didn't say anything to me. They didn't tell me to go to work on the farm or anything; I had my job. That's why I don't really like washing my clothes nor cooking. I would go far out to hunt.

---

175. Añuje, or *Dasyprocta punctata*, a large, edible rodent closely related and similar in appearance to the lowland paca.

176. Quirquincho is the Bolivian common name for the armadillo, *Dasypus* sp., called carachupa in the Madre de Dios region. Don Ignacio mentions bringing back "its full weight" because armadillo is especially enjoyed cooked in its shell, which makes cutting the animal into pieces in the forest a less attractive option than returning with the whole animal.

There's a fruit there called manchingo.[177] There's tons of it there. That tree bears its fruit, which the collared peccary, the white-lipped peccary, and the deer eat. I would look to see where the fruits had been browsed over the most; that's where I would climb up high. Suddenly a deer would be coming close, see, and *boom!* That was the end of that deer. It's heavy, that one. I would leave it there, cover it up with leaves there, and then I would say to the old man, "I killed the deer."

And he would go to bring it back. I would tell him where it was and he would bring it home.

I once killed two deer at a feeding place by a large stream. The water was crystal clear and there was a tight curve in the stream, just like in this river here. There I went, I popped out there, and the deer is right there up close. Why wouldn't I kill it? I loaded my shotgun and I killed two. Why kill more? I left them there. I went to let the old man know with my brother—I had an older brother. They picked them both up, they carried them. I couldn't carry them, though I could carry a collared peccary.

Here, there's no game. Here, you can walk all night and you won't find a thing. Not over there in Bolivia, there the paca's as plentiful as mice, the jochi pintado. That's what my life was like before, when I was a kid. Now I feel bad about killing animals. If I kill one peccary, that's it, I don't kill any more. Before, I used to kill everything I could carry, but not anymore. I wonder why. Now I feel pity about killing the poor little guys. Even more so if it's a monkey. I feel pity for them when they're looking back at me.

I once took my son, Sixto, hunting. We went to the Gato,[178] we entered the Gato, which is a large stream. We came to a fork in the stream and that's where we stopped.

"This is where we'll sleep, damnit. We're staying here," I told him.

It must have been about three, or maybe two in the afternoon.

---

177. The manchingo fruit of course comes from the manchinga tree, *Brosimum alicastrum*, described earlier.
178. A tributary of the Tambopata River.

"Let's go. We'll head this way," I tell him.

We got to an aguajal; the aguajal was all cleared out from the white-lipped peccaries having passed through. We tried to cross the aguajal but it was just more water, then more water.

"No, a boa could grab us."

So we turned back. Then I tell him, "You'll see how tame the monkeys are here." I say to him, "They'll come in an instant."

I imitated them and they answered, "*Aaah!*" The monkeys came, two massive ones. They were two males. They're watching us and start to shake the branches. Sixto was watching how the two of them were shaking the branches.

"Shoot it," I tell him.

"Poor thing!"

He feels pity, he says. He was eleven years old, I think, and he already knew how to shoot too.

"Shoot it!" I tell him.

"I feel bad, poor thing."

He shot it: *bang*! The monkey falls down, there's the monkey, dying, going *heeee, heeee.*

"Poor thing, why did we kill it?" says Sixto.

I feel sad about killing it. I feel pity for the monkey when I kill it, yes indeed.

The healthiest monkey is the howler monkey. That one doesn't have a single worm in its stomach. That one eats ojé leaves; those fools cure themselves. And the tapir eats patiquina and really any kind of herbs, which is why sometimes a person with leishmaniasis gets irritated from eating its meat. But tapir and monkey meat are the best, the howler monkey and the tapir. Those animals don't have any worms or anything; they're healthy as can be. Meanwhile, the black monkeys, white monkeys, spider monkeys, they have worms as long as spaghetti right now in the dry season. That's why I don't really like spider monkey. You have to serve it a purgative.

Roasted caiman[179] is tasty too, its tail. Do you know how to cook a lizard? You smoke it with lots of salt. You're not going to eat it right then. Leave it for the morning. Boy, is caiman smoked overnight tasty! Once we caught one with a hook when I was a caiman hunter,[180] three fishhooks shaped like this, a G turned in on itself. We'd hang a pava carcass or half a monkey from it and just leave it dangling there. Then he comes over and *boom!* We found one that was the biggest, four meters seventy, almost five meters. Geeze what a brute of a beast! There's no way two people are gonna be able to pull that ashore. You can't drag it. We skinned it; we pulled the hide off, my brother and I. Its tail weighs more than its body, and behind, on top of its tail, there's a thick part, double like this. That's what we would fry. We would catch two, three, four in a night. We brought back caiman oil, you see, like four cans. It's good to take for the lungs. We fried it, made fried chunks of it. You can eat it nice and hot, but cold you won't want to eat it. It has a nasty aftertaste then. That's what that one's like.

---

179. As is common in the region, Don Ignacio refers to the caiman here as a "lizard" (*lagarto*).
180. Don Ignacio makes reference to an era when caiman hides were an important regional extractivist industry and caiman hunting a trade.

Tamamuri
Brosimum acutifolium (Moraceae)

There are two types of tamamuri: large-leafed and small-leafed. The small leaf kind is a remedy for lower back pain and all that, and the resin is to fortify the blood. You bleed it and drink half a cup of it. Its water is sweet; its milk, it's creamy, delicious. It's sweet. You can diet it if you want to, and it's better that way, or if not, just diet it one day, two days, and you're done. The other type is no good as a remedy but its fruit is tasty. With that one, you chop down the tree, you leave it there for two days, and on the third day you come back and the whole branch is ripe; delicious.

    I heard the man that raised me talking about it, but I don't know how he prepared it. I guess he cooked it. This one, you drink a cup of it and get drunk; and two boys will go and take care of you, behind you in the darkness. That's when the plants will teach you, what it's good for, everything, and those boys will accompany you. I say that the bark has to be boiled, you let it ferment, and then you take that and diet it.

Tahuaironga
Rhipsalis sp. (Cactaceae)

Tahuaironga is a plant that grows up high and is like an onion,[181] it hangs down. You harvest the straightest ones. If you want, you can take it mashed up, just rolled up with tobacco and then you swallow it. Or otherwise, you cook it along with ayahuasca, like you do with chacruna, and that makes you walk above, up high.

Topa →
Ochroma pyramidale (Malvaceae)

The bud of the topa (balsawood) is good for treating scabies and mange. It's spicy, that one. Spicy, but its aftertaste is nasty; it's not tasty.

---

181. Here Don Ignacio compares this epiphyte's long, thin, succulent-looking stalks to the long leaves of onions or scallions (*cebolla china*).

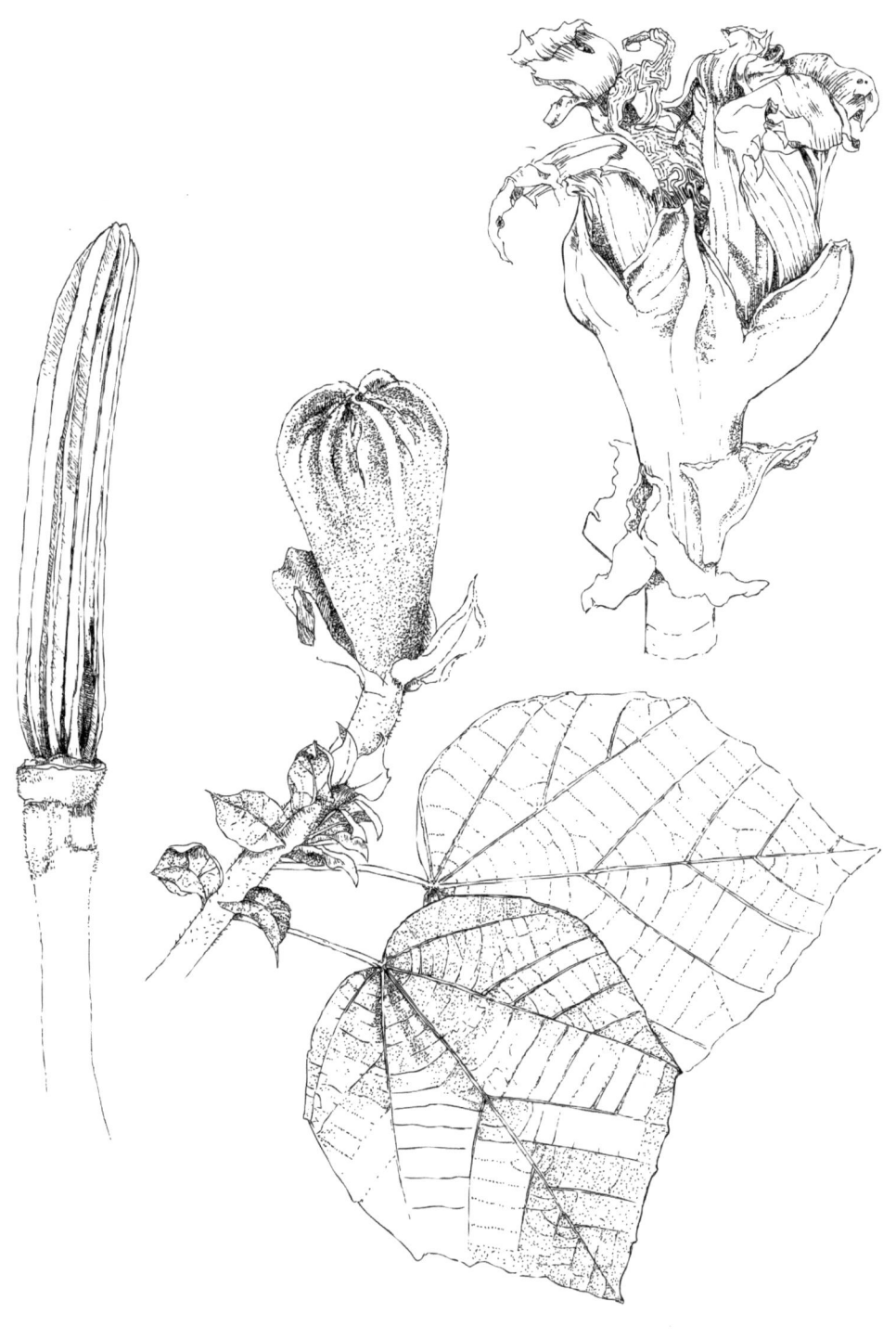

Tongoy Sacha
Vasconcellea sp. (Caricaraceae)

You bathe with it in the new moon to get rid of all the "salty bad luck" that you have on your body; all the curses, the bad vibes that you have on you, because sometimes you might have lots of people saying, "That guy is a piece of work," or, "He's a terrible bastard." This plant gets rid of all of that.

Ucuyucui Sacha
Zanthoxylum sp. (Rutaceae)

Ucuyucui sacha is another one to bathe yourself with, but it has two names. The name used by the indigenous is contesa, I think, but here we call it ucuyucui sacha.

This one is to bathe yourself for protection from brujos. Its leaf is like "mouse tail," like verbena; do you know verbena? It's like that; it's a bit smelly. It's used boiled; bathe yourself with it in water as hot as your body can stand.

I used to have bad dreams; sheesh. And over there in the bajío floodplains, you'll find these. Its little flower is smelly, and when you pluck it, your eyes will burn. I already knew of some patches of it; I brought it, see, and laid it out in my bed. That one's great for defense.

Yarina →
Phytelephas macrocarpa (Arecaceae)

Yarinilla
unidentified species

There's an herb, yarinilla, which grows stuck to tree trunks. You pull it down from the heights, you fold it and peel its little heartwood. You take it out and pour water on it; as you're peeling, it'll color the water like tea. That one is for the little ones, for anyone; you give it to them as a tea, just a little bit. It's good for diarrhea, dysentery, all kinds of things, even for babies. And for the mothers that have trouble breast-feeding it's good too; it won't harm her in any way. It's a lovely plant, a climbing plant; its leaf is like a little palm tree.[182] It's a vine.

---

182. The palm tree referenced is yarina, from which the plant name of yarinilla is drawn (meaning "little yarina"). The yarina in question is *Phytelephas macrocarpa*, source of so-called "vegetable ivory," hard seeds often carved and utilized in traditional Amazonian handicrafts.

Zarzaparrilla
Smilax officinalis (Smilacaceae)

Zarzaparrilla (Amazonian sasparilla) is good for the kidneys; you drink it by the little shotglass-full. You have to diet it, because if you don't diet it, you'll have white blemishes appear on your skin. You could end up all "spotty-spotty". Just with food, keeping your diet properly, that's the hardest part. You don't eat garlic, onion, papaya, beef, pork, skin fish; you can only eat scale fish.[183] When you stop taking it, you have to keep to your diet at least a month.

---

183. Amazonians often divide fish into two general classes, scale fish and skin fish. The latter class includes all manner of catfish and dorado, which are considered to be incompatible with most plant diets.

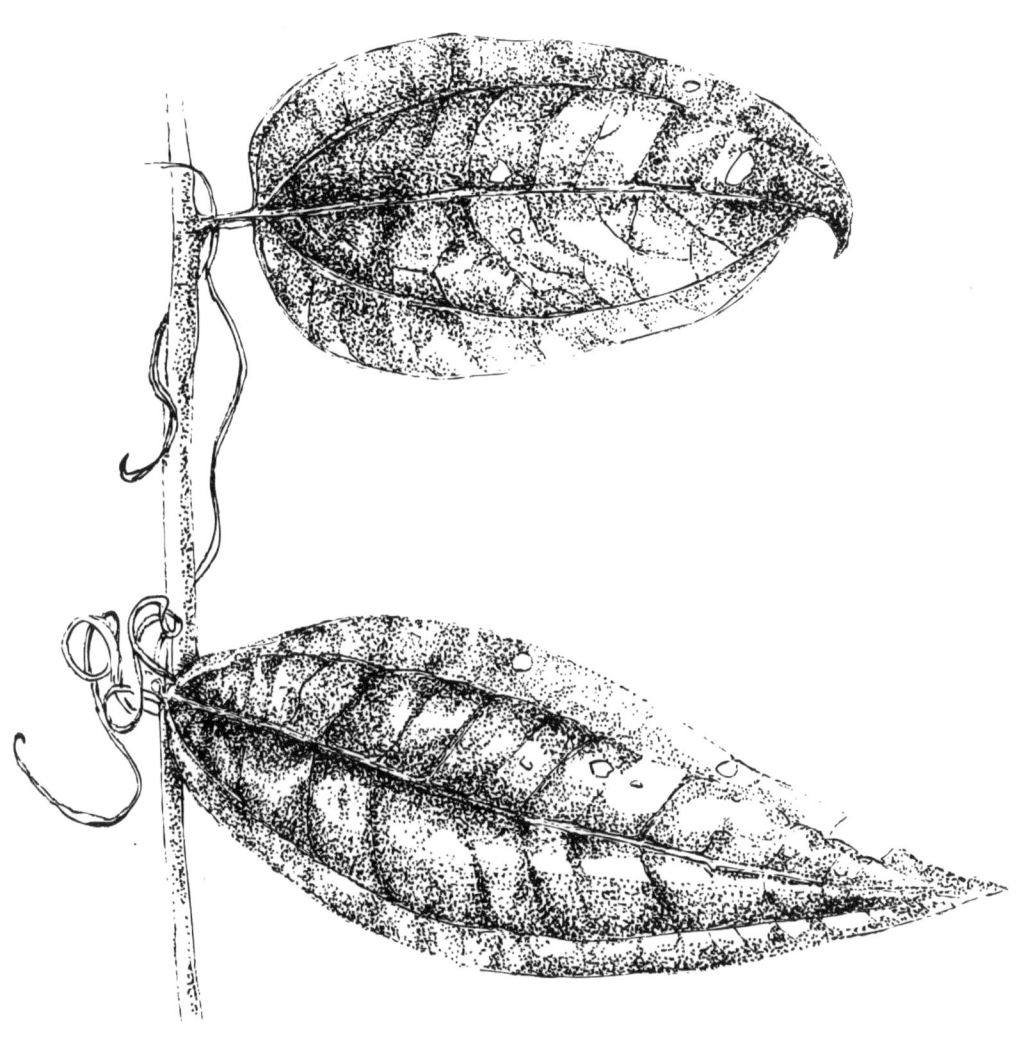

TWENTY-SEVEN

The Painted Tiger

I have eaten tiger, but the red one.[184] There's one thing, though: they say you can't eat the jaguar that has eaten dogs. How is that? Because they become fierce when they eat dogs; they no longer respect people anymore.

I was going around the Malinowksi in that time when we were working the hide trade. On the beaches of the Malinowski, I was searching for a jaguar and couldn't find it; we never managed to find one! No matter what, it couldn't be found. There were its prints all along the beach, but we couldn't find it. The jaguar has never confronted me; he's scared of me.

I killed four tigers here; with a dog I killed three jaguars. I had a dog that caught jaguars, damnit; you can spot a dog that will be a jaguar hunter. One of them, I killed at night here; his head was right next to me, looking at me like this.

When this was all forest, the road over there was just a path. And over there, past the school, there was someone from the community who was building his house there; and there was another dirt road too where we would cross over that side. And one day I say to the mother of my children, "I'm going out to walk for a bit." I tell her, "Maybe I'll find a paca."

So I went over that way, I went in via the path. There's a fork a bit further down; I'm shining my flashlight that way. I don't know why it occurred to me to shine it to the side, and there's a puma,

---

184. Jaguars and pumas (mountain lions) are often referred to in the Peruvian Amazon as tigers: painted tiger (*tigre pintado*) and red tiger (*tigre colorado*), respectively.

watching me, his head up like this, watching me. I shot him right there, *pew*! That's where I left the fool.

I got back here and the mother of my children had heard the shot. "What did you shoot?" she asks me.

"I shot a red tiger; I left it there groaning," I tell her. "We'll go and see it in the morning."

She had a brother; the next day I say to him, "Let's go see the puma."

We went in the morning to see and it wasn't there. Where it lay was still warm; that's all.

"You go this way, I'll go that way, listening," I said to him. "It must be over there somewhere, complaining."

I went along a little ways; that's where it was, laid out. They had chopped down a caimito,[185] and it was hidden among the fallen tree's branches.

"Hey, come over here; it's here," I tell him.

We climbed over the branches; there it was, moaning. I shot it, and we left it right there. It was going to pounce on me; that's why it was looking at me that way, from close to the ground, his head down, watching me, that's how it was bracing itself, with its rear end sticking up.

Do you know what happened to that lady in I don't know what lake, down there? The lady was going to her farm patch to get some yuca at like ten in the morning; she was by herself, you see. And there was a tortoise[186] on the path; she kept walking and a jaguar starts coming her way. The jaguar was sitting right there. She shouted at it and it wouldn't go away; it just moved its tail. Then, she threw the tortoise at it but the jaguar remained there; then it started coming toward her. And what did she do? She gathered courage, and when it jumped on her, she managed to get on top and grabbed it by its front legs. It had made her drop her machete too. And the lady was trying as hard as she could to reach the machete, riding it still, keeping hold of the jaguar, until

---

185.   Tree, *Pouteria caimito* (Sapotaceae) with delicious fruit and nice, reddish timber.
186.   Motelo, yellow-footed tortoise (*Chelonoidis denticulatus*).

she reaches where the machete is. She grabs it and stabs both of its eyes and then shoves the machete into its mouth, but it had scratched her all over; it had bitten her hand here. So she stabbed both of its eyes, let go of it, and that's where the jaguar remained, dying. She ran home, and her compadre was there. Like me, I guess, he was a veteran.

"Compadre, a jaguar has scratched me! Go, find it! It's going to come here any minute, it's coming!"

The man grabbed four shotgun shells and set off. The bastard is coming, following the scent. He shot it with the four shells, killing the jaguar. They loaded the woman onto a boat and took her to Maldonado as an emergency. That's what I call being brave, eh? Not just anyone does that.

Hot Pepper, Ají (*Capsicum chinense*) →

TWENTY-EIGHT

Animals and Their Secrets

I t's this way with animals. Before a pregnant lady is at three months, if she looks at a donkey, that boy will come out well-endowed; if she looks at the "weaponry" of the donkey, you see. She should eat the huancavi,[187] the expecting mother; she should eat that kind of little animal before her three months of gestation, so that when any kind of insect stings the child, it won't have any effect on him. A snake can bite him and it doesn't have any effect either; all those things, because that bird eats nothing but small vipers up in the treetops. Let her eat it any way she wants; boiled, or even better if roasted. And the babe will come out with that power, that it won't affect him or her at all if they get bitten. Whether it's a bite from the bullet ant, a scorpion, or from a snake, he won't feel any pain. All those animals, like the giant anteater,[188] eating all those meats, then there's no kind of insect that will affect him. That's why I'm the way I am; I got three snake bites and I didn't feel a thing. My mom talked to me about it; that's why I put my faith in that, you see.

Scorpions, do you know what they're good for? You find a scorpion, you cut its tail off, and you take it and scrape your arm

---

187. Bird of prey known in English as the laughing falcon or snake hawk, *Herpetotheres cachinnans*. This species is most known for its habit of eating poisonous snakes.
188. Oso bandera, giant anteater (*Myrmecophaga tridactyla*). Just as the huancavi eats poisonous snakes, the giant anteater eats ants, including bullet ants, without any apparent pain. Don Ignacio suggests that eating the meat or taking the broth of these animals during the first trimester of pregnancy can confer to the unborn child the same resistance to venoms and pain seemingly enjoyed by these animals who subsist on such poisonous animals.

with the tip of its tail. It will really heat you up, though; and don't get close to a fire for four days. When you throw a punch, you'll leave the other's eye all red and black for a month. That's that one's secret; that's the scorpion's power.

As for the monkey with spines,[189] you take its fur off; you could say they're spines. Remove a small amount and boil that, and have patients suffering from that illness take it—epileptics. A man told me about it, and so I tried it with a friend that lives with the daughter of my *comadre*;[190] I prepared it for him. I prepared him a small bottle, one of those soda bottles, and the guy got better; he got better. You just drink small cups of it, early in the morning and before going to bed; those are its indications.

Then there's the lard of the giant anteater, but you have to be in the sun for that. You lay out a sheet, a mattress, some leaves, whatever, right in the sun. You have to be in just your underwear; get them to rub it all over you and you stay there in the sun. Then the person that is helping you comes to massage you, to rub you all over. With three healings, you'll get rid of all the pains, so they say, with giant anteater lard.

---

189. Don Ignacio refers tongue-in-cheek to the bicolored-spined porcupine (*Coendou bicolor*), locally called cashacushillo, as the *mono espinudo* or "spiny monkey," in consideration of its arboreal lifestyle, not so unlike a monkey's.
190. The mother of his godson (female equivalent of compadre).

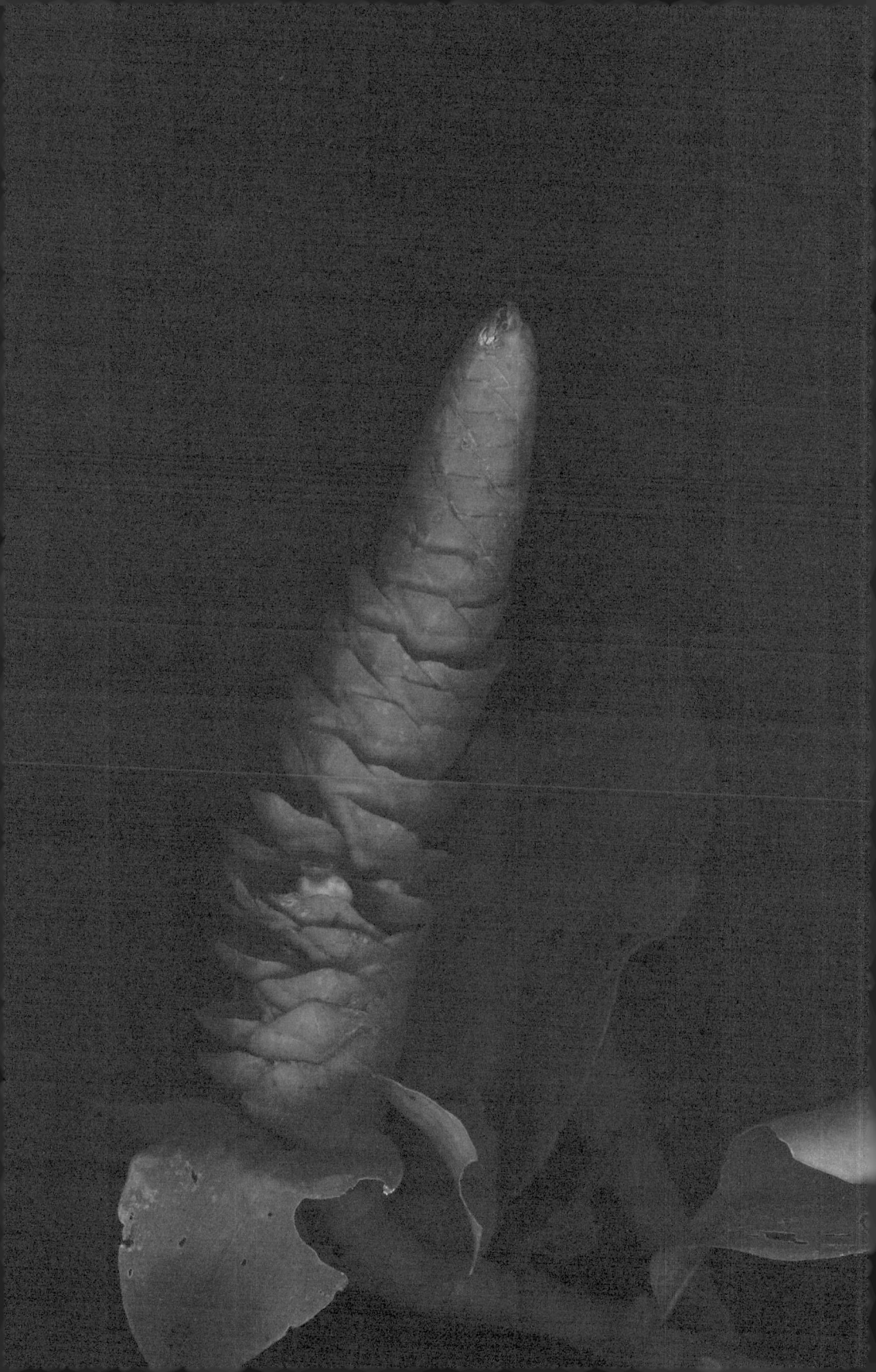

TWENTY-NINE

The Old Ones

I met a lady from Pucallpa. Silveria Vásquez was her name. That lady knew when a sick person would arrive.

"Today at five in the afternoon, a sick person will show up."

And they would arrive, they really did. She smoked her cigarette rolled in banana leaf. The people would arrive, and she looked them over.

"Your son doesn't have any life left in him," she would say to a person. "He's going to die at such and such a time."

And she would get it right, what she said. Well, that's real knowing, isn't it?

The old ones, they truly did know. They would tell you, they would look at you and say, "Do you want to be with so-and-so? Do you want her to come over right away?"

They worked on you at night and eight days later the girl was with you. They sure did know! Because the old ones lived in the middle of the jungle. Here among the populace, it's difficult; you have to be far away from any audience. And they would come out from there and they couldn't be around small children; by just looking at them, smiling at them, the little ones would get sick. That's what it was like before. Not now. Now we haven't really learned. We only know a little bit; we don't know anything. The remedies, too, we don't know them. Apprenticeship now is not like it was before.

← Caña Caña (*Costus* sp.)

I'm corrupted too, these days. Right now, I don't diet ayahuasca properly. What I have going for me is that I don't have a wife. That's the only thing I've got going for me, because if I had a wife, Jesus Christ would have already taken me. I won't let myself be taken by just anyone. But I want to escape death. When death comes for me, I'll escape to Tres Chimbadas,[191] and death won't find me.

---

191. Tres Chimbadas is a lake found within the territory of the native community of Infierno.

Bobinsana (*Calliandra angustifolia*) →

Epilogue

On the last day of August, 2019, in a modest gathering in Puerto Maldonado of people who knew and loved Don Ignacio Duri, we came together for the launch of the first (Spanish) edition of this book with little pomp or fanfare. It was a tranquil occasion, and with his 89th birthday celebrated just mere days before, Don Ignacio was softspoken in front of these people he had known for years. After all, it wasn't like Ignacio to boast, and so he accepted the congratulatory hugs graciously and, by early afternoon, was accompanied back home by his eldest daughter.

Less than a year later, Don Ignacio passed away, two months before he would have reached his ninetieth birthday. He continued to receive and treat the sick and needy in his home through to the very end of his life. The book you're holding, the book he had envisioned and spoken of for years, was born of an intention he had, to leave something of his knowledge behind when he would inevitably pass on—especially since he didn't have a direct heir practicing healing in his twilight years. A principle of Ignacio's that he expressed on multiple occasions was to "not be stingy" with one's knowledge, to share what one knows freely as a show of humility and a proof of virtue. And so, he proposed to me one day to set things down on paper, to tell his stories, that his life of familiarity and close apprenticeship with plants might continue to be of service to others, to the common good.

Service was his vocation. He was selfless and hardworking as few are. In total he spent thousands of sleepless nights holding vigil over the transformational experiences of people he'd never met before, often people he'd never see again after. On more than a few occasions, he put down his dinner plate before taking a bite in order to serve medicine to a surprise last-minute arrival, even if he hadn't eaten all day. Yes, as he mentions in passing in these

← Coca (*Erythroxylum coca*)

pages, he was generous almost to a fault. Grateful participants in his ayahuasca ceremonies sometimes left him with cash payments that for his village's standards amounted to considerable windfalls. But often the next day his pockets would be empty again, after yet another of his rounds around the community to contribute to the wellbeing, the emergencies, and the tragedies of others with stoicism and kindness of the rarest form.

It was a great kindness that he paid me, to welcome me into his home for around a year and a half, from 2004 to 2005, as his sons and daughters and grandchildren also graciously did. Often sleeping on the floor or in a hammock, I got to witness directly the diversity of his patients and their complaints, and Don Ignacio's incredible endurance and commitment to his vocation. My time in his home was one of the great highlights of my life, something I will always return to in my thoughtful hours. These are memories worn from affectionate use: the long days shared in a canoe on the river; and out in the forest, Ignacio's intelligent, quizzical gaze scanning the greenery and reading things in it that I couldn't even begin to discern. In the years following my time as a porch squatter and water bucket carrier in his home compound, I would often stop back in to visit, bringing him a thankful rack of plantains from a little farm patch I managed upriver, sometimes sticking around for a night or for a week.

On one of those visits, after I'd known him for years, Don Ignacio started telling me out of nowhere about a book he was seeing. At first, I thought he was describing a vision or a dream, in which his vast knowledge of plants had been magically preserved in the form of a glowing book, an "illuminated" manuscript full of visionary luminescence. I remembered the sweet visual metaphor he used to share with listeners on his porch, of the forest as an old-fashioned pharmacy wall with shelves and shelves of remedies. For one with vision as clear as Don Ignacio's, you could look at the forest and make out the medical indications corresponding to each plant—and even their price, in terms of diet required in order for the cures to work. And so I imagined Ignacio's "book" lit up as another vision he'd had of the divine nature and origin of healing plant knowledge, just like his pharmacy.

But he persevered on me that this wasn't (only) another dream symbol; it was also an earnest, tangible step to share freely of the knowledge he carried about medicinal plants, which he often humbly claimed was limited at best. In reality, Don Ignacio's ecological knowledge was encyclopedic, though also cryptic. His custom in life was to be sparing with words, though when the mood struck him he could be charismatic and loquacious. He would run to both the ends of that spectrum of shyness and effusiveness over the years in our interviews, recorded on a small digital audio recorder, with all the rooster crows in the background and neighbors dropping by to interrupt and ask for a favor.

While Don Ignacio desired to leave behind something of his knowledge, he also realized in the telling that many of his stories and tricks of the trade were really more of value to those actively engaged in learning with plants. And, as evidenced in Ignacio calling his work "occult science" on more than one occasion, he didn't consider esoteric guidance for those actively dieting plants—as a teacher would instruct the student—to be public teachings. With the recorder running and a broad audience in mind, Don Ignacio was selective about what he wanted to share for inclusion in the book.

Strange, almost magical healing can occur via the grace of plants and their mysterious processes. Don Ignacio was the first to point out that the plants, and not he, were the ones really doing the healing. Ultimately, like all great herbalist teachers, Ignacio wanted to inspire his students to learn directly from the plants, through dieting, dreams and ayahuasca, just as he had, getting to know for oneself the plants' lessons, learning to call them in and sing their songs—and paying the real price, going the virtuous road, of long diets and hard-earned knowledge.

Ignacio often invited participants in his ceremonies to sing if they felt inspired. He would hand them the sanganga leaves tied together with a rubber strap that he used in ceremonies like a maraca and invite them to sing. Sometimes he'd sing at the same time someone else was singing, and the effect was mesmerizing. Don Ignacio's songs were moving, gorgeous, beautiful. Some were aching and some rang out "like little bells." *If you can sing,* he'd say, *sing.* And if you can learn, learn. More than an attempt to exhaustively share his complete pharmacy—unique to him and to his relationships with particular plants—the desire of Don Ignacio was to open the door and invite others in. To do their own diets, that nobody can do for them, with their own plants. To form their own relationships with plants as special as the many he describes here, whose songs he knew well and sang so beautifully.

It's a sorrow for the world he left behind that his voice will make those songs sound no more. And yet, here, he has left us a small piece of his voice that we can still continue to hear.

—*Robin Van Loon, Puerto Maldonado, 2022*

Achiote (*Bixa orellana*) →

Acknowledgments

The authors thank: Antonio Fernandini, Cristian MacDonald, Neftalí Fernandez, Roxana Povea, Augusto Daddario, Osman Octay, Pierina Zlatar, Oscar Miró-Quesada, Cindy Miró-Quesada, Luz Marina Duri, Luis Duri, Elicena Duri, Sixto Duri, Silverio Duri, the Native Community of Infierno, Indira Llerena, Patricia Burgos, Xavier Escudero, Jhony Aragón, Javier Bórquez, Michel Saini, Miwa Bankova, Francisco Aros, Andrés Flandez, Carolina Gutierrez, Elizabeth Contreras, Elías Candia, Olivia Revilla, Manuel Huinga, Piher Maceda, Varun Swami, Campbell Plowden, Nicholas Hardy, Jennifer Zackin, Adolfo Ibañez, Vanessa Frias, Gina Vela, Julio Araujo, Laurie and Eric Van Loon, and Elisabeth Lagneaux.

This edition exists thanks to the efforts of the non-profit organization Camino Verde. For their material support, thanks to the Marjorie Grant Whiting Center for Humanity, Arts and the Environment—and to all those who contributed to the grassroots crowdfunding campaign for the book.

Special gratitude to Blair Butterfield and Maisie McNeice for their plant portraits (Blair) and botanical illustrations (Maisie). Additional big thanks to Blair as a key collaborator on the book's creation in various crucial ways. And to Elise Van Der Heijden, for helping this long overdue English edition be born.

Thanks to all those who supported this book in so many ways, via opinions, reviews, and words of encouragement. And to all the many whose names we have left out, all those who appreciated and loved Don Ignacio.

← Don Ignacio harvesting chacruna (*Psychotria viridis*)

Don Ignacio's house in the Native Community of Infierno ↑

Don Ignacio Duri Palomeque, in 2014 →